HOW TO BE
EUROPEAN

Travellers' Joy

HOW TO BE EUROPEAN

Compiled by E. O. Parrott
and edited by Noel Petty

Illustrated by W. F. N. Watson

S I M O N   &   S C H U S T E R

LONDON·SYDNEY·NEW YORK·TOKYO·SINGAPORE·TORONTO

First published in Great Britain in 1991
First paperback edition published by
Simon & Schuster Ltd in 1992
A Paramount Communications Company

Copyright © E.O. Parrott and Noel Petty, 1991
Illustrations © W.F.N. Watson 1991

Simon & Schuster Ltd
West Garden Place
Kendal Street
London W2 2AQ

Simon & Schuster of Australia Pty Ltd
Sydney

A CIP catalogue record for this book is
available from the British Library
ISBN 0-671-71157-1

Typeset in Palatino 10.5/12.5 by
Falcon Typographic Art Ltd, Edinburgh & London
Printed and bound in Great Britain by
Billing & Sons Ltd, Worcester

W.F.N. Watson first had illustrated humorous articles and cartoons published during his thirty years' Regular Army service.

Since he retired, his maps, historical illustrations, humorous verse, prose and artwork have appeared in thirty books. From 1977 to 1988 he was question-setter for the television programme University Challenge, and also wrote for other television programmes.

CONTENTS

ARE YOU READY FOR 1992?

As the Year of the Single European Market approaches, many public figures can be heard lamenting Britain's unreadiness for the challenges it will bring. Large sections of industry, they tell us, are oblivious of both the commercial opportunities and of the competitive threats; among the general public, confusion reigns.

There is a paradox here, for in our travels about Britain, as we shall see, we have found everywhere a goodwill and enthusiasm for the concept of being European – albeit not always well-directed. What was missing, it seemed to us, was a sound textbook for the apprentice European. This book aims to supply that need.

Our team of correspondents has therefore been despatched all over Europe, sending back reports on places and people, on customs, cuisine and culture. The aspiring European, if he applies himself diligently, should be able by the end of this book to claim common citizenship with Mozart, Molière and Michelangelo; to be, in short, a European.

First, however, we would like you to take a little time to complete a brief questionnaire. Keep a record of your answers so that, when you retake it after you have finished the book, you will be able to see how much more European you have become.

1. Is 1992
   a)   a heavy-metal rock band from Newcastle?
   b)   a new telephone code for London?
   c)   when trade barriers drop all over Europe?
   d)   a recently-discovered novel by George Orwell?

2. Is the Single Market
   a)   a cut-price dating agency?
   b)   the promotion company behind the Eurovision song contest?
   c)   another plan for re-developing Covent Garden?
   d)   a simpler way of selling goods and services in Europe?

Cut-price Dating Agency?

3. Is the EEC
a) a patent sting-relief, particularly effective against wasps?
b) a poisonous food additive used to colour soft drinks?
c) Steven Spielberg's latest film about an endearing alien?
d) a way of encouraging European trade, so that Spanish onions end up in Scunthorpe while Stilton cheese gets to Strasbourg?

4. Did Britain join the EEC in
a) 55 B.C. (a result of the Roman invasion)?
b) 1066 (After the Battle of Hastings)?
c) 1815 (as part of the Romantic Movement)?
d) 1973 (as a last resort)?

5. Did Britain join the EEC for
a) cheap wine?
b) a chance for Mr Heath to broadcast in French?
c) a new outlet for rioting football fans?
d) the amusement of lots of civil servants who thought the shuttle to Brussels would have more style than the 8.05 from Godalming?

6. Is Britain's biggest benefit from the EEC
a) easy shopping trips to French hypermarkets?
b) an influx of scantily-clad foreign language students?
c) a reduction in the number of civil servants on the 8.05 from Godalming?
d) the chance for lots of magazines to print quizzes like this?

7. Is Mrs Thatcher's attitude to Europe
a) hatred: because Mr Heath got all the publicity by getting us in?
b) contempt: because it's all foreign?
c) envy: because *their* Royals take the back seat?
d) superiority: because they're not British?

8. Is Mr Major

a) pro-Europe because all the best Plazas in Spain are named after him?

b) nostalgic for bread and circuses?

c) prepared to take whatever action is appropriate if and when the right circumstances occur, always bearing in mind and paying due regard to . . . ?

d) confident because neither Herr Kohl nor Monsieur Mittérand can tell a leg-break from a googly?

9. Is the Labour Party's attitude one of

a) nervousness because Mr Scargill has been seen reading 'Say It In French'?

b) uncertainty about whether to ally itself with the Christian Socialists, the Socialist Democrats, the Democratic Christians, or the Scottish Episcopalians?

c) embarrassment about having to take the Internationale seriously?

d) hwyl?

10. Is or are Brussels

a) a night club founded by Bertrand Russell?

b) a fruit or a vegetable?

c) a perfectly harmless town in Belgium that wasn't hurting anybody?

d) the place you wouldn't start from if you were trying to get to Strasbourg?

11. Will the Channel Tunnel

a) flood?

b) enable rabid squirrels to race over from France and infect our household pets?

c) increase demand for ladies' underwear at all branches of Marks & Spencer south of the Thames?

d) ever be finished?

12. Do most people in the EEC speak

a) French?
b) loudly?
c) loudly, *and* wave their arms about?
d) English, in desperation?

EEC-SPEAK

a)   b)   c)   d)

13. Finally, should we celebrate 1992

a) with a year-long street party?
b) with champagne?
c) with a bang?
d) with a whimper?

So how European are you?

If your answers are mainly **a)**s you obviously haven't a clue what's happening around you but enjoy life and parties. So, why not get over there and take a look at what Europe's up to.

If you've ticked more **b)**s than any other letter you don't know much either, but have got a good eye for nubile young Europeans, and probably own a dog. Don't use him as a excuse for not going over there – the kennels can open tins of dog food just as well as you.

If most of your answers are **c)**s you take a more detached view of the Single Market. You've heard of it, but you'd rather it stayed 'over there', and that the Channel Tunnel remained a castle in Spain. Try harder!

If you've totalled more **d)**s than any other letter, please keep your views to yourself. We're in this up to our necks and the last thing anyone wants is people like you blowing the gaff on the Emperor's new clothes. Please.

D.A. PRINCE

EUROPAEANS

*The first thing the aspiring European should note is that Europe
is no longer to be defined in terms of continental shelves, land
masses or tectonic plates; it is now an Ideal. Before we descend to
the particular, therefore, the Eurostudent should spend this first
chapter contemplating Europe as a whole, in all its simultaneous
unity and diversity.*

Bliss it is to be alive now,
Euro-dreams at last come true,
Never year so hyped and hoped for,
Hail to Nineteen-Ninety-Two!

See the Famous Twelve in concert
Entering the Promised Land,
Merging in the Single Market
Euro-visionaries planned.

Whom Commerce hath joined together
Let no politicians part,
Trade does more than wishful thinking
To give Europe a new heart.

From the Wash to the Aegean
Hidebound attitudes are shed,
We must learn that Britain's moat is
Not the Channel but the Med.

This *annus mirabilis* now
Ushers in the Age of Gold;
What new hopes lie round the corner?
What else does the future hold?

What ideas will sprout from Brussels,
Chunnelling beneath the Straits?
Shall we soon be jingling *écus*
In the new Eunited States?

Critics may complain that there is
Less incentive now to roam,
See no point in foreign travel
When Abroad is just like home.

Banish all such petty carping,
Let the banners be unfurled,
And the trumpets sound a welcome
To our Brave New Euro-World!

STANLEY J. SHARPLESS

Cultural Stereotypes Rule O.K.

In Spain the path of Time is never straight;
It arches like a tropical banana.
The Spaniard's motto is 'Procrastinate:
Neglect today what you can do *mañana*'.
In Italy men brashly stare and lurk,
Their hands plunged deeply into trouser pockets.
Invisibly, their fingers are at work,
As though to prise their gonads from their sockets.
The Germans' love of discipline and order
Is world-renowned, as is their record score
At crossing some adjacent nation's border
With nothing to declare but total war.
The French extort the foreign tourist's francs;
By nature they are grasping, mean and rude.
They grab all they can get, and give no thanks
(Although their chefs create fantastic food).
Cuisine in Belgium doesn't count for much
(The Belgian joke is chips with everything),
While Luxembourg clips coupons and the Dutch
Are squeaky-clean and decent but lack zing.

The Scandinavians are clean as well,
Although the magazines they print are dirty.
They pay high rates of tax. They ski like hell.
They suicide. They're mostly under thirty.
Our European partners – what a soup:
The blond, the swarthy, soap- or garlic-scented,
Nasal and guttural, a chequered troupe,
Quite alien to us. And quite demented.

BASIL RANSOME-DAVIES

WFMW

A European Alphabet For Absolute Beginners In 1992

A's for Albania, Marx's last mate,
B is for Belgium, a rather small state.
C is for Cyprus where Greeks fight with Turks,
D is for Denmark where Hamlet's Ghost lurks.
E is for Eire where snakes are unknown,
F is for France and the wines of the Rhône.
G is for Germany, now all in one,
H, by analogy, stands for the Hun.
I is for Iceland with geysers and cod,
J is for Jersey where money is God.
K is for Knowledge of new things to eat,
L is for Luxembourg, Justice's seat.
M's for Monaco, the playground of lords,
N is for Norway that's riddled with fjords.
O stands for Offshore and oilwells awash,
P is for Poland and *Solidarność*.
Q's for the Queerness of Boche or of Frog,
R's for Romania with orphans to flog.
S is for Spain where crooks live in peace,
T is for Turkey, but watch the police.
U's for United, which one day we'll be
V is for Vatican, Peter's Wee Free.
W's for Wales, where guards follow a goat,
X is the Cross that we use when we vote.
Y's Yugoslavia, a racial mish-mash,
And Z is for Zlotys and other strange cash.

JOHN SWEETMAN

Hail to Europe

In between the steppes of Russia
And the northern herring pond,
To the south of arctic hush, a-
Bove the Nile and lands beyond,
Here is Europe, the receiver
Of all different types of race,
Nordic cool to latin fever,
Clout teutonic, celtic grace.

So, all European nations
Stand together side by side,
Leave behind all confrontations
Let your aims be unified,
Set aside all trade embargoes,
Regulate your subsidies,
Build up mountains from your cargoes
Higher than the Pyrenees.

Where Napoleon and Nelson
Fought to gain supremacy,
Let us fight for nothing else on
Land which is forever free.
Where de Gaulle with gallic humour
Made a point by saying 'Non!'
Let each EEC consumer
Thrive on affirm-ation.

Where the British stooped to conquer
Then puffed up with their success
Made the Chancellor a plonker
Keeping out of EMS,
Let each treasury be willing
To accept the Eurosnake,
Subjugating franc and schilling,
Pound and deutschmark to its shake.

Let no rancour taint your dealings,
Never show self interest,
Think about the others' feelings,

Never say your Country's best.
Dampen patriotic fever,
Sublimate all native pride,
Take all measures to achieve a
Europe that's solidified.

Spreading, growing ever greater,
Let your numbers swiftly swell,
Till your members can create a
Strong invincible cartel.
Closer, ever closer blending,
Melt all lines of sovereignty
Till the world knows it's contending
With the glorious USE.

KATIE MALLETT

EUROPLACES

In this chapter we aim to give a taste of some of the places in Europe that the novice European should see first.

The Costa del Sol

Say goodbye to your tantrums and tension:
From the day you're receiving a pension
   You can have a long hol
   On the Costa del Sol
With pleasures too many to mention.

Say hullo to the blonde on the pillion
And the bottles of booze by the million;
   I'm sure that senescence
   Can beat adolescence
In painting the city vermilion.

Say goodbye to your Qses and Pses;
For a greybeard can date whom he pleases;
   And then if he's lucky
   She'll say he's a Ducky
And welcome avuncular squeezes.

Say hullo to the sun and the beer, oh!
You can pose to the world as a hero,
   And no one will boo you;
   At least, if they do, you
Can turn down your deaf aid to zero.

PAUL GRIFFIN

I fear I cannot paint you without rancour
The Costa Brava and the Costa Blanca.

PAUL GRIFFIN

Rome

The Vatican, the Vatican
we wandered there and back again
from Via Julius Caesar you
turn right and you are at it then;
the marketeers are everywhere
you pass them by, and Peter's Square
is to your right and through the gate
you find the fountain and you're there.
The guards in fancy dress stand by
(they carry weapons, God knows why)
but don't waste time go on until
the Sistine Chapel takes your eye.
A rapid glance will quickly show
the famous Michelangelo
preoccupied with lots of nudes,
you heave a sigh, and off you go.
Museums, chapels, painted crypts –
the oohs and ahs assault your lips,
fantastic to have been and seen,
but now you're set for other trips.
(Forget the bloody fish and chips!)
The Spanish Steps you've got to view,
the Trevi Fountain beckons you,
get on the metro, no great feat,
and see the Colosseum too.
There's Trajan's Column, goodness me
It's time to travel to Capri . . .

FRANK McDONALD

The Loire, with its famous chateaux
Is attractive as far as it geaux,
But, compared with the Seine,
I would firmly maineteine
It's a second rate dreine – and it sheaux!

MICHAEL FOSTER

In Venice it's hard for a tramp
To set up an overnight camp,
For St Mark's Square submerges
Each time the tide surges,
And the streets are exceedingly damp.

KATIE MALLETT

The tower of Pisa keeps leaning
A bit more each season, this meaning
That soon it will lie
Parallel with the sky.
(Which will make it more easy for cleaning).

KATIE MALLETT

In Père Lachaise Cemetery

For wormy circumstance, try this:
Stroll down the titled avenues
Of Paris's necropolis
And count the corpses where they lie
In family sarcophagi –
Expensive, gothic, bleak
And sheltering an underclass
Of bristling, feral cats who streak
Like radar blips across the grass
From all invading shoes.

Apollinaire, Bizet, Colette,
David and Eluard: the names
Encode a marble alphabet
Of French – of European – art,
Though dimmer bones, too, play their part –
A strangely mingled crew:
The duellist of little skill,
A mad philosopher or two,
And buried mediums who still
Drag out their occult games.

The corner for the Commune dead,
A wall-flanked wedge of quiet terrain,
Is history's ground, for where you tread
Was where a different future died
In rituals of fratricide . . .
Elsewhere, scrawled signs read 'Jim':
The raver's gravestone is the place
Their arrows lead to. Yes, it's him,
A chipped, graffiti-smeared stone face.
The children are insane . . .

Now contemplate the Déco sphinx
That guards the tomb of Oscar Wilde.
There, *hubris* went before a jinx:
He mocked the ways of boring pseuds
With Anglo-Saxon attitudes

And paid, in spades, the price.
Should old Britannia boldly go
To swell the party, break the ice
And join him in a *fine à l'eau,*
Will he be reconciled?

BASIL RANSOME–DAVIES

A Villanelle from Tuscany

Just fancy launching boats from here –
  Real boats, I mean, not pedaloes!
They've changed the beach of yesteryear.

Put down that empty can of beer:
  Someone will clear it, I suppose.
Just fancy launching boats from here.

No lonely dips these days, my dear;
  ICES FOR SALE, the notice goes.
They've changed the beach of yesteryear.

Old fishermen and nets and gear
  Were there, where tubby ladies pose;
Just fancy launching boats from here.

Some tiresome birds beyond that pier
  Would nest where all that housing grows:
They've changed the beach of yesteryear.

The locals hate the atmosphere;
  Efficiency gets up their nose.
Just fancy launching boats from here:
They've changed the beach of yesteryear.

PAUL GRIFFIN

Fancy launching boats from here!

The Brandenburg Gate

Oh, Brandenburg, for long the gate to hell,
The living death of deprivation's curse
Before the wall around you swiftly fell
To let the hungry millions traverse
The border to democracy and wealth,
Unfettered by the communist ideal,
And not by exercising midnight stealth
But freely walking through. How do you feel,
Isolated after many years?
Now just a monument to Prussian power
And symbol of a severed nation's tears
You may well ask, in glasnost's shining hour
As by your side graffiti's ugly spore
Spreads Wogan's name, 'Is this what freedom's for?'

KATIE MALLETT

In the Catacombs

'Are any actual corpses buried here?'
the American asks with middle-aged persistence.
The youthful English guide is growing weary
of his charge's baseball-capped resistance
to information given three times already.
'There've been no bodies here for centuries,'
he reaffirms, his voice crisply steady.
The American shakes his head, screws up his eyes.
'No corpses. Gee. What in hell's this place for?'
Fists thrust into pockets, he strides unbent
where centuries of pilgrims knelt to adore.
Traipsing past emptied tombs I am content –
albeit the saints and martyrs aren't at home:
in August this is the coolest place in Rome.

TOM AITKEN

The Ariège

The tourist maps display a blank
Where no one goes to tan or ski;
A weathered, hidden Arcady
As hard and natural as a plank.

The houses in the mountain cloud
Have walls the shade of fishes' scales;
Above the nimbus, waymarked trails
Web out to spread the hiking crowd.

A village Sybil whispers how
A summer swarm of men on bikes
And cars and cameras and mikes
Obscured the pasture from her cow.

'The age of speed' – what she was taught
Was simply that what touches fits.
Her grandson lives in Biarritz,
As distant as an astronaut.

It doesn't pay to stay and farm,
The slopes assume an altered face
Of barns with baths and parking space
Whose *maquillage* is rustic charm.

Sheep ramble on the forest floor,
As lifeless as an ammonite,
Where conifers conceal the light.
The lorries grind. The chainsaws roar.

Tough Spanish loggers fell the pines
And cart the cut wood off to Spain,
Which trucks it back to France again
As standard furniture designs.

What special sense of wonder crowns
This chain of peaks that irrigate
A shallow, green collection-plate
And power its money-coloured towns?

BASIL RANSOME-DAVIES

On Being Lost in Venice

I'm sure we crossed this bridge not long ago.
We turned out of that brick-built colonnade
with plaster medallions, set oddly low,
studding its walls. And then we must have made
for the spire of the church we're hoping we might see
along this fondamenta, through that square
beyond the grim-faced statue and those three
small shops. The spire's in view, right there,
behind the locked-up, gaudy-with-posters block
which could be flats. We went that way last time.
Let's try through here, startling this warbling flock
of scavenger pigeons. An archway, low. Green slime
edging the water. This time . . . surely . . . ? No!
I'm sure we crossed this bridge not long ago.

TOM AITKEN

Munich

In Munich there's held every year
A knees-up with brewed atmosphere,
Where chaps dressed in leather
Keep dancing together –
They SAY they're just there for the beer!

KATIE MALLETT

Florence

A maiden aunt visiting Florence
Might view with a certain abhorrence
Nude statues galore
With parts to the fore
Which art, she'd maintain, never warrants.

KATIE MALLETT

Drawbacks of the Mediterranean

One curse of the Mediterranean
  Is a longing to plaster and paint,
To put on a wing, or a floor, or a thing
  That might be a garage, but ain't.
No building they start's ever finished;
  With all the improvements they do
You're constantly baffled by pieces of scaffold
  When you're trying to get into the loo.

There are curious insects in Italy,
  And specks in the salad in Crete;
The average walker in Rhodes or Majorca
  Will be stung from his head to his feet.
There's a noisy mosquito in Cyprus
  That drives you near out of your wits;
How did Aphrodite get out of her nightie
  Without being bitten to bits?

But the Med has a magic that conquers:
  The ointment is more than the flies;
When the sea is all sheeny and ultramariney
  It's a sight for the sorest of eyes;
And the sun on the thyme and rock roses,
  The olives and carobs and vines,
The air oxygenic, Hellenic, Edenic,
Make the whole place so scenic and non-neurasthenic,
  That the critic is lost and resigns.

PAUL GRIFFIN

APHRODITE
KALLIPUGOS

Paris

A fellow, by name Gustav Eiffel
Had an urge, that he just couldn't stifle,
To build a huge pylon
With steel by the mile on –
The ultimate souvenir trifle.

KATIE MALLETT

Your Questions Answered:

Q. Why was France originally called Gaul?
When early tribes inhabited what is now known as France, they imported with them the habit of smoking pungent tobacco-sticks, known as 'Gauloises'. Because of this notorious tendency, the region was christened 'Gaul'. The modern name 'France' derives from the *franc*, or coin, which was used (ironically enough!) to purchase the Gauloises. Later still, the coin gave the language of the Gauls its proper name – *lingua franca*.

Q. Why are the Benelux countries so called?
The word derives from Latin, *bene* (good) and *lux* (soap), and refers to the obsessive cleanliness of the denizens of Luxembourg, Belgium and Holland. In these countries, the streets are scrubbed daily at dawn, schoolchildren wash their faces three times during a school day, and all milk is specially filtered by a local preacher, or *pasteur*.

Q. Why is Holland known as The Netherlands?
Because the literal translation, The Nether Regions, was felt to be liable to cause offence.

Q. What is the importance of The Hague?
The Hague is where World War I finished and was named after Douglas Hague, the British commander. It is where croquet is played with the traditional croquet potatoes. The Orange Order is decided upon there. It is where the International Jurists sit. There are twelve of them, and they can be called up any time to decide on important legal tussles – for instance whether a Bourbon is a biscuit or a drink, whether spanking should be permitted if the child consents, whether you can wear

... the traditional croquet potatoes

a mini in the Midi, and vice versa, whether masochists have the right to self-determination, who the Saar of Germany is, whether the Côte d'Azur is blue, whether Britain should return the dominoes stolen by Lord Elgin, and if it is safe to wash in the Paris Basin.

Q. What is the origin of the phrase 'Rome was not built in a day'?

This interesting old saw refers to the cartographical problem of *suburbia ex pande*, that is, that it is impossible to chart the growth of a city because, as soon as the chart is made, it is obsolete. And yet the original Rome WAS built in a day, by itinerant Picts and shovels. Ramparts were thrown up, villas constructed, a hot bath installed, all within one frantic twenty-four hour period. Unfortunately, this original settlement was near the outskirts of modern Bordeaux, owing to a misunderstanding about specifications. It was subsequently rebuilt near Palermo, Nicosia, Glastonbury and Baden-Baden before work began upon the current site. Hence also the saying 'All roads lead to Rome'.

BILL GREENWELL

EUROCORNERS

In a short book such as this, the Eurostudent cannot expect to cover the full panorama of all that Europe has to offer, and we will inevitably spend much of our time in those countries which are both the most prominent and the closest to Britain. However, we must not forget the host of smaller or more peripheral countries which also form a part of our rich heritage. This chapter is devoted to them.

Albania!

There's a corner of the Med that's been forgotten,
It's on the Adriatic, north of Greece,
A place I've never been to, but one day soon I mean to
Take a ticket and indulge this odd caprice:

I've got a mania for Albania,
I can hear it calling from afar,
It's cut off from the West,
That's why I like it best,
And no one there's allowed to have a car.
Albania, Albania,
My Baltic Ruritania,
I'll get zanier and zanier till I'm there;
Oh, how I'd love to jog
Through the land of ex-King Zog,
And consummate this long-range love affair!

STANLEY J. SHARPLESS

Finland

A curious country is Finland:
It's a mixture of thick land and thin land,
   For all round the coast
   Is where the land's most,
While the water is plentiful inland.

PAUL GRIFFIN

A Dream of Portugal

When I was just a little lad of not much more than ten,
Our geogger teacher told us things that seemed quite
      useless then.
But still one fact stays with me from those days of chalk
      and talk:
The chief exports of Portugal are port, sardines and cork.

A little later on in life I learned the ways of Trade,
Of billion pound computer deals; how power plant is
      made.
I thought it then a trifling thing beside such vast machines
To deal in merely cork and port and Portuguese sardines.

But now in riper years I see that all is vanity;
The finest things we find in life, though not exactly free,
Are not high-priced technologies, but things less dearly
      bought,
The simple things, like Portuguese sardines and cork
      and port.

One day to Portugal I'll go, and on some beach I'll walk.
Beside the sea I'll eat sardines, and slowly draw a cork
To wash them down with crusted port, and find out what
      Life Means.
In Portugal, the land of cork, and port, and tinned
      sardines.

NOEL PETTY

Turkey-in-Europe

It's no longer a gamble
To visit Istanbul
Or gaze at the hills of Gallipoli.
You can visit the Black Sea
By boat or by taxi
And soak in it, African hippo-ly.

You'll be wanting to hear
Of Mersin and Izmir
With their temples in groves of acacia,
But through no fault of mine
We're drawing a line
At the Bosphorus, boundary of Asia.

It's Europe, I'd mention
That holds our attention
And Asia must stay unexpressed,
So, after one starry-
Eyed gaze at Scutari,
We must turn our face back to the west.

PAUL GRIFFIN

Your Questions Answered

Q. *Is Monaco in the Common Market?*
This is a very tricky question indeed. Monaco is a sovereign state, run by the Grimaldi family who used to star in the circus. However, Monaco is very friendly with France, and France, of course, is part of the Common Market. Monaco probably *will* join one day but, during the War, the Germans attacked their capital, Monte Casino, and broke the bank. This, I am afraid, has not been forgotten.

Q. *Is Andorra a country? What is it like?*
Yes and no. Andorra *used* to be a country, but it no longer exists, having been swallowed up by France in a sudden *coup d'état* in the 1960s. This was not good news for its main industry which, as with many other small

countries, is stamps. It is mainly famous for its Andorra goats, out of which so many famous coats have been made. Andorra had no language at all, which of course made the region unspeakable – hence the takeover.

Q. Is Liechtenstein in Europe?
Indeed it is. This tiny country has been made famous by Robert Maxwell, who keeps his money in it. It is a very small country indeed, consisting as it does of one large building with a series of signs announcing 'Passports', 'Cashier', 'Foreign Transactions', 'Customer Advice Services Management Supervisor' and 'Exit'. The shopping is limited. Although it is not formally in the EEC, it is thought to own most of it.

Q. Where and what is San Marino?
You do not need much Italian to translate the name of this wonderful little country. Literally, it means 'Holy Sea' – a phrase most curiously misspelt in Britain as 'Holy See'. In other words, it is where the Pope (who presides over Europe's most tiny state, the Vatican) goes for his summer holidays. Set amidst glorious sands before a pellucid azure sea, San Marino offers friends and Romans everywhere a fresh, new, inspiring and frankly mystical experience. We cater for small children and also grandparents too! Come and see our fantastical stamp collection, or simply sit back and soak up the atmosphere. See the famous Stanley gibbons! [This answer was paid for by the San Marino Tourist authority.]

Q. Is the Isle of Man in Europe? Who is the Dame of Sark?
The Isle of Man *is* in Europe, like all the Channel Islands – Guernsey, Jersey (where the sweaters come from), Ynys Mon, Wight, Mull, Lindisfarne, Scilly, and Dogger Bank. All of them have their own police force, and have revived the ancient fertility custom of 'birching', which is very jolly.

The Dame of Sark is an entirely imaginary figure. 'Sark' is just a place in a famous poem by Lewis Carroll called 'The Hunting of the Sark', which concludes that 'A Sark was a Boojum'. Possibly 'Dame' arises from the corruption of Boojum into *Begum*, or 'mportant woman'. Incidentally, this is the origin of the Northern expression 'Eee ba gum' – i.e. 'Dear mother of the family'.

BILL GREENWELL

EUROLIT

One of the most effective ways to become European is to read the works of English language writers of the past, who have always been enthusiastic travellers.

English Writers in Europe

English writers, like many other artistic types born on these shores, commonly live as far as possible from their place of origin. Most of them go no further than Europe, though Robert Louis Stevenson popped up in the South Seas — strictly on medical grounds, of course — and anyway he was a Scot.

It is surprising what grounds can be discovered for going to the most heavenly place one can imagine: in the thirties a whole batch of writers went to Spain, ostensibly to interfere in a war; Browning pleaded his wife and his father-in-law as an excuse for settling in Italy; and Byron explained to the Countess Guiccioli he was there to avoid scandal. I am not sure what Shelley was explaining — perhaps that he was looking for Byron.

Even Isherwood's plea that he was in Germany to be a camera was less than the truth, which is that these writers went where they wanted to go because they wanted to go there. We who manage fourteen nights bed and breakfast in a half-built tower block on a dirty grey beach once a year, have long gazed in envy at the writers in their villas, high above our mean affairs: Paddy Leigh Fermor in Southern Greece, Larry Durrell in the Midi and, earlier, Noel Coward on his Alp with Robert Graves perched on a crag in Majorca.

Perhaps the day will come when we too sit in the friendly sun by our swimming pool, sipping Pernod and passion fruit, writing immortal lines about the beauty of the country to which nothing on earth would persuade us to return.

'Meadows of England, shining in the rain!' wails James Elroy Flecker, fresh from a swim in the Bosphorus. 'Oh, to be in England, now that April's there!' sobs Browning, between gulps of Campari.

In reverse, continental writers hardly ever settle in this wonderful England, unless they are genuinely in fear of their lives. No one suspects Karl Marx of a sentimental passion for the British Museum Reading Room.

European literature does not need England; but clearly, without Europe, English literature would cease to exist. There would be nowhere to write it.

PAUL GRIFFIN

It is tempting to wonder how some of our writers might have responded to the Europe of 1992.

Abroad Thoughts from Home

(Br*wn*ng)

O to be in Europe
Now '92 is there,
And waking up to Europe
Means we're totally aware
That our tariff bars and Customs posts
Will soon be dead as ancient ghosts
As the Single Market shows us how
In Europe – now!

And '93 – what then will follow,
What more can fall, or Europe swallow?
Look, where the franc and lira, pound and mark

Rub shiny shoulders, and o'er-weigh the pocket,
'Til Euro-travellers, fumbling, loud remark
If common coinage comes, they will not mock it.
A policy some view as – not with rapture! –
The first fine hairline fracture.
And though the EC's rough on member states
Who, out of line, oppose its stern dictates,
Its bureaucrats, Brussels' grey-petalled flower,
Will smooth each gaudy diff'rence with their power

D. A. PRINCE

Euro-Cargoes

(M*s*f**ld)

Gleaming silver monster on a long-haul flight path,
Forty thousand feet above the Alpine snows,
    With a cabin full of rich men, first-class travellers,
Waking up to bubbly from a long, cool doze.

Scheduled flight from London, zooming out to Germany,
Serving mostly Seltzer and a light Moselle,
    With a cabin full of yuppies, British and American,
Checking on their briefing for the next big sell.

Battered little Boeing, heading into Malaga,
Working at a profit for a cut-price line,
    With a cabin full of school kids, housewives, burglars,
Getting pretty squiffy on the free white wine.

PAUL GRIFFIN

Ode on the Dawning of the Single European Market

(McG*n*g*ll)

At last – 1992!
The year about which there's been such a hullabaloo.
After a lot of difficult negotiations
No fewer than 12 different European nations
Now form a Single Market, stretching from the silv'ry
    Tay
As far as Greece, which is quite a long way.
Henceforth travelling on the Continent will be so easy
The idea need no longer make one feel queasy.
With over 300,000,000 customers at our door,
We should be able to export a lot more,
And so become a good deal better off,
A prospect at which it would be foolish to scoff,
Though with all this new competition there is no doubt
We shall certainly have to pull our fingers out.
What a good thing Britain joined the EEC,
Otherwise I don't know where we should be.

If Scotland had been counted separately, as it should
    have been,
Instead of 12 countries there would be 13,
However, that is something which for the moment we
    must shelve,
So to be going on with, let us give 3 cheers for the 12!
As for what will happen next, who can say?
We shall just have to live from day to day.

STANLEY J. SHARPLESS

A Tourist's ABC

(Al*r*c W*tts)

An Altrincham art-class, awfully arrayed
Bravely by Baedeker besiege Belgrade.
Couriered coachloads camera-clad come,
Diligently detailing Danube's drearest dome.
Every entablature eager eyes explore
For friezes, fillets, foliate finials four.
Great gadrooned gables gawping gazers greet –
Homesick, hotelbound, hating humid heat.
Illyrian ices? Incipiently ill
Jane jostles Justin, Jeremy jogs Jill.
Kitschiest keepsakes Kulturkinder kid,
Like 'local' leadware ('Longton' labelled lid!).
Many mugs mint Marks, market merchants muse.
Nightmares nag news-nuts, (nobody needs news).
Optional outings oldsters overtax;
Puny pickpockets pinch purses, passports, packs.
Querulous questioners, quintessential queues,
Rustic restaurateurs refunds refuse.
Sliwowicz sampled, Serbian sights surveyed,
Thirty tired trippers taste the tourist trade.
Uplift unforgettable? Urlaub unsurpassed?
Varied vacation – vistas very vast –
Well, wasn't wet, (was Watchet, Windsor, Wells?) –
Exotic excursion – experience excels –
Yes, Yugoslavia! Youngsters, yachtsmen, you
Zealots zoom Zadarwards – Zounds! Zagreb Zoo!

GAVIN ROSS

Death in the Discotheque
(H*m*ngw*y)

There are people who will tell you otherwise, but if you wish
to study the art of *juliganismo* you should visit Torremolinos.
I have seen the fights in Madrid and Cordoba, but there it
is done with a lack of passion and, afterwards, a feeling of
shame. Because there is no serious intention to damage,
the element of physical danger is absent. Also, often the
fighters are not drunk enough or else they are too old. But
in Torremolinos there is always the danger that comes with
cheap wine and the presence of many young, violent people.
It is important that much wine be drunk because, although
many are sick, the art cannot be performed with the brain,
and if you are a an intellectual with a deficiency of the male
parts *juliganismo* is not for you and you should stay away.

The fighters spend many hours in ritual preparation so that
the action commences late, but for the *aficionado* this time is
not boring. You can tell much about the fighters from their
preparation, such as that the one who drinks too quickly,
and may seem truly aggressive, has no stomach for the
bodily harm and extensive destruction of property that are
the special beauty of *juliganismo* and will not, later, assault
anyone but instead will utter sexual insults to young women.
There is an art to the uttering of sexual insults, but it is a stale
and empty art, like the paintings of David Hockney, and there
is no sense of threat to it. Really, anyone can do it.

In the Disco-Bar Wham in 1983 the Essex Pistols fought
with a classical rigour for seven hours and sent twelve
people to hospital, including a Guardia Civil. There were
serious mutilations and, I believe, a severed jugular, though
I am unable to swear to this on account of the vomit. It is
hard to see details when your head has been vomited on, and
some do not like the vomiting part, though without it there is
only a sterile formalism and no test of nerve. Dave Dork, the
Wanstead boy who fought five seasons in Torremolinos, one
with a ruptured spleen, would vomit on himself. The smell
was formidable, the vomit and the unwashed clothes and,
sometimes, double incontinence, all that and the lack of air,

the loud music, the furniture disintegrating, everything a blur, a panic, and, invariably, cries of pain.

Then too, the police would intervene, not in a pedantic fashion to restore order, but to hit, themselves, the fighters who were attacking one another and, after the intervention, the police, so that the violence was general. Of course the police had the advantage, as they were less drunk and did not have to stop all the time to vomit, but art is not a matter of fair play and besides it is sad. I do not think I have seen anyone as sad as Dave Dork. His sadness was of a great depth and after he met the woman he was sadder and I knew he would never be any good again.

BASIL RANSOME-DAVIES

The Isles of Greece

(B*r*n)

The isles of Greece, the isles of Greece
Are now within the EEC,
And Homer nods and rests in peace
When Brussels-based bureaucracy
Decrees the wine-dark sea should take
The status of a wine-filled lake.

D.A. PRINCE

Duty Done

(P*m A*r*s)

I thought I'd write one of me poems
In praise of the EEC,
But it's turning out rather different
From what it was meant to be;
I can't feel enthusiastic,
'Cos there's one thing bothering me.

I'm afraid that the Single Market
Is going to be a flop;
So far as yours truly is concerned,
It's really not much cop.
(And you won't get me through the Tunnel
With all that water on top).

The thing that'll stop me going
On those cheap-day shopping sprees –
And though it hurts me to say so,
It's the fault of the EEC's –
They're actually going to do away
With the cut-price duty-frees.

What's the use of going
To the Calais Super-Marché

If you can't bring back cheap plonk and cigs
In the good old-fashioned way?
You might as well shop at Tesco,
At least, that's what I say.

No more need to wonder
What the cross-Channel fare is.
No more Brie and Camembert
And cream from those nice French dairies.
Calais is written on my heart
Like it was on Bloody Mary's.

I'm staying put next Christmas,
Deaf to the family pleas,
No more trips to the Continong
Though they beg on bended knees;
I'll splash out on some Gucci shoes
What I save on me duty-frees.

STANLEY J. SHARPLESS

Grantchester Reversed

(Br**k*)

. . . God! I will pack and take a train
And travel Europe once again.
The EEC's one group I know
Where common-passported I'll go:
And Brussels sprouts in every heart
A love of bureaucratic art,
And European pulses beat
At new directives on spring wheat.
The French appease their bourgeois dreams
By lavish dining at Maxim's.
In Italy society's café-er
Except when threatened by the Mafia.
While Eire men know just what sin is –
A publican who waters Guinness.

Each man in Portugal's José
And only sups Mateus Rosé.
The Spaniard talks a lot of bull
And tipples by the wine-skin full.
The Luxembourgers are a bunch
Who close the country down for lunch.
In Holland there is none so erring
As he who does not swallow herring,
While gallant Belgium shows us ways
To smother chips with mayonnaise.
The German diet's wurst and torte:
Their sugary wines resemble water.
Of Denmark there's no notice taken –
Their sole concern is slicing bacon:
And Greeks, the latest in the arena,
Wash down their sorrows in retsina.
Touring the EEC goes jammily
Now we're all one big Euro-family,
And every instinct bids me stir
From Cambridgeshire and Grantchester,
From sludgy mead and reedy fen
To ramble Europe once again.

D.A. PRINCE

Euro-if

(K*pl*ng)

If you believe the French are rather charming,
If you're convinced that Belgium is unique;
If you find Germans wholly unalarming,
(If you adore the language that they speak);

If you regard the Danes as quite exciting,
If you think every Greek a decent chap;
If Luxembourg to you seems most inviting,
(If you can even find it on a map);

If you deem all things Dutch to be exquisite,
If you admire the Irish for their style;
If Italy to you seems worth a visit,
If Spain and Portugal you don't revile;

If, be they chic or perfectly plebeian,
To hobnob with these nations makes you glow,
You'll be a quintessential European,
And possibly the only one I know.

RON RUBIN

Albert Goes to Paris

(M*rr**tt *dg*r)

One weekend, young Albert Ramsbottom,
  'Im as ad trouble wi' lion,
Took a notion to travel to Paris
  To look at that tower built of iron,

It seemed that 'is teacher 'ad told 'im
  About Common Market and such
And said: 'Now we're all Europeans
  It's right that we should keep in touch.'

So as it were young feller's birthday
  They packed up and straightaway went
On a ferry from Dover to Calais
  On sightseeing pleasure 'ell-bent,

But when they clapped eyes on the marvel
  That yon clever Eiffel 'ad made
Father Ramsbottom said: 'Crikey!
  That really puts ours in the shade.'

You see they were all born in Blackpool
  With its tower that's both famous and tall,
And to see summat bigger and better
  Didn't please the Ramsbottoms at all.

But 'as it 'appened, our Albert
  'Ad with 'im a lovely big set
Of Meccano 'e'd 'ad for 'is birthday,
  To play with if weather turned wet,

And inside the box were a tool-kit
  For tightening up nuts, bolts and screws –
An item that Albert was certain
  Was one 'e was going to use.

That night 'e crept out of his lodgings
  All secret and stealthy and sly,
And sneaked out to where Eiffel Tower
  Soared up in't Parisian sky

And, being a smart little nipper
  Who'd worked out just what 'e must do
He dismantled that ruddy great structure
  Down to the last nut and screw.

He dismantled that ruddy great structure

Then they stuffed it in sacks and departed
   For home on the very next tide
And halfway across English Channel
   They chucked the lot over the side.

And that's why if you go to Blackpool
   And mention the subject of towers
Folks there 'll say: 'Cop that one yonder
   It is the biggest there is, and it's ours!'

PHILIP NICHOLSON

A Song Against Europe

(Ch*st*rt*n)

When God laid out our planet,
Millions of years ago,
Britain was joined to Europe,
As fossils clearly show;
Later, upon reflection,
The good Lord thought it best
To separate us, seeing
We're different from the rest.

And so, through countless aeons,
He re-arranged the scene,
Deliberately inserting
The Channel in between,
So that God's Englishmen
Could dwell for ever free,
Securely set apart
By wog-defying sea.

Whom God hath put asunder
Let no man seek to join;
Boycott the Channel Tunnel,
And alien ecu coin!
Beware the Euro-dogs –
Dread carriers of rabies –
Ready to rush across
And bite our English babies.

United States of Europe?
The whole thing is a con
By faceless functionaries
In Paris, Strasbourg, Bonn;
Once-happy Brits are now
Betrayed by zealous fools,
We used to rule the waves,
But now they've waived the rules.

We won't drive on the right,
We won't give up our Queen;
Pardon, M'sieu – we'll stay
The way we've always been;
Here is a piece of wisdom
For every Eurocrat:
Good fences make good neighbours;
Kindly remember *that*.

No hectares and no kilos,
We love our English pound,
No garlic and no nonsense,
We won't be pushed around.
God save us from a Europe
By men of Brussels planned,
The bureaucratic nightmare
Of their Cloud-ecu-Land!

STANLEY J. SHARPLESS

A Song for Europe

(Any Eurovision Songwriter)

Pop into your travel bureau,
Everybody's going Euro,
That's where we belong;
Once you get as far as Calais
You'll find everyone so pally-
On the Continong.

(Chorus)   Cheers! *Prosit! Santé! Ciao!*
Kiss both cheeks and make a bow,
We are all *amigos* now,
Cheers! *Prosit! Santé! Ciao!*

Yoo-hoo-hoo, it's Ninety-Two,
The year when all our dreams come true,
Sing it far and wide;
Say goodbye to British phlegm, dear,
Let yourself go – be more like *them*, dear,
On the other side.

Kiss both cheeks

Cheers! *Prosit! Santé! Ciao!*
etc.

And make a bow

We'll go dancing cheek to cheek,
Whisp'ring love in Euro-Speak,
Happy days before us;
And wherever we may be
Venice, Brussels, Bonn, Paree,
We'll sing this Euro-chorus:

Cheers! *Prosit! Santé! Ciao!*
                              etc.

If there are occasions when you
Cannot understand the menu
On one of our trips,
There's no need for parley-vooing,
(That may lead to your undoing),
Ask for fish 'n' chips.

Cheers! *Prosit*! *Santé*! *Ciao*!
                    etc.

Seeing famous Euro-places,
Meeting friendly Euro-faces
Every single day,
We shall be so Euro-smitten
That when we get back to Britain,
This is what we'll say:

Cheers! *Prosit*! *Santé*! *Ciao*!
                    etc.

STANLEY J. SHARPLESS

Barcelona

*(K*pl*ng)*

From the summit of 'is column, 'ighly on-parade and
        solemn,
Chris Columbus casts 'is eye across the town,
Watchin' bands of 'appy amblers down below 'im on the
        Ramblas,
Givin' glad-eyes as they saunter up and down.
In the boozers they serve dishes 'eaped with little foreign
        fishes
What you eat with toothpicks, not with knives and forks,
And your Catalan is 'andy when it comes to swiggin'
        brandy
But most of all the 'eathen devil talks.
'E will serenade your lug'oles with the story of 'is strug-
        gles
Or the goals what Gary Lineker 'as missed.
You can bet your bleedin' kitbag 'e'll say: 'Franco was a
        shitbag'
As 'e makes a filthy gesture with his fist.
While your local colour's speakin' there's a never endin'
        shriekin'

From a fruit-machine what's perched atop the bar
And your ears are gettin' clouted by the orders bein'
    shouted
By customers 'oo want another jar.
All the racket from the traffic jammed outside is somethin'
    graphic,
Like an 'ore's 'owl when your rubber johnny's torn:
You can 'ear a thousand curses from the drivers, and
    what's worse is –
Their sweaty 'ands is never off the 'orn.
What with sirens, bells and 'ooters, and the noisy kids on
    scooters,
And the poundin' from the club what never shuts,
It's a fair old ding-dong riot. Still, 'oo fancies peace
    and quiet?
All matelots are Barcelona nuts.

BASIL RANSOME-DAVIES

Dog End

(H*rry Gr*h*m)

When Uncle bought a dog abroad,
He ill-advisedly ignored
The statutes and the regulations
Governing such importations.
So Aunt and Uncle died of rabies,
Revoltingly, with all their babies.

RON RUBIN

EUROTRAVEL

There are many ways to see Europe. The simplest of all is the package holiday, bought through your travel agent.

Florence,
Wednesday.

Got here yesterday, nice digs, leave tomorrow. Do you know what, Fred, you remember that plaster statue of a nude bloke that Auntie Edie won at the Bingo, the one she kept hidden under the stairs? Well, we were just strolling out for a bevvy last night when I turned a corner and here it was in the square, large as life – well, twice as large, really – and nothing missing, if you know what I mean. They call it David here. I'm not kidding, these Italians will rip anything off.

Regards to May,
Charlie

Siena,
Thursday.

Arrived here this morning, and got quite a shock. We were just looking for the loos when we were swept into the middle of the town by a enormous crowd. Would you believe it was a horse-race? Right there in the middle, like having greyhound-racing in Trafalgar Square. Well, you know what the Italians are like, it was seething mad. The 4.15 at Newbury it certainly was not. I couldn't get a programme, not to mention a pork pie and a glass of Watneys and to cap it all they gave the race to a horse that had thrown his jockey three laps back, with no stewards' enquiry or anything. Good job I never got near a bookie.

See you—
Charlie

Venice,
Thursday.

Quite a nice place this, but dead easy to get lost, and if you happen to be on the wrong side of the road, it costs you a quid to get across. Last night we wandered into a big square with a queer-looking church at one end. We saw a sign that said Caffe Florian so I naturally thought you could get a cup of coffee for a florin. When we'd finished – nice cup, I will admit – I offered my 20p and the waiter wanted £5! I was for calling the police, but Beth thought they might be in on it, so we paid up and left. Apparently Florian is the owner and it's famous or something. What a liberty!

Charlie

Strasbourg,
Sunday.

You won't believe this, but the people here are called Alsatians. Honest, no kidding! They eat like Alsatians, too. Last night we had something called a shoe cruet, a sort of huge cabbagy mass stuffed with bacon, sausages, pork and God knows what. In the top of it they'd stuck a pink, fleshy object about six inches long. I said they wouldn't would they but Beth said oh yes they would they'd eat anything and wouldn't stop giggling. I don't know what the lads at the Arms would have made of it, but we left it well alone. The courier told me today it was the pig's tail, that straightens out in the cooking. Phew!

Cheers—
Charlie

Tours,
Tuesday.

Beth says that Tours is just the name of this town, but it sounds like a smart piece of marketing to me. Anyway, we took one of their tours – a cruise up and down the Loire. Quite interesting, too, one or two nice brick and cement works, several fertilizer factories and a really smart nuclear power plant. Unfortunately they kept stopping the boat to let people off to look at some big old houses they have dotted around – I suppose they used to belong to the factory owners. Still, it was a nice change from all the history.

Regards to Ned and the regulars at the 'Arms'—
Charlie

Chartres,
Wednesday.

Stopping off here on the way to Paris. Not much of a place, I don't know why they chose it – more or less like Woking but with a big old church in the middle. There are some huge stone figures round the doorways, thin as beanpoles. Beth says it's because there wasn't much to eat in the old days, but they're supposed to be kings and suchlike so it can't be that. I expect it was just the fashion at the time, like the F-Plan. Still, you can see where that bloke Lowry got his ideas from. Paris tomorrow!

Charlie

Paris,
Thursday.

Well, here we are! Beth says it's the capital of European civilization, but I can't quite see it. They do have a Marks & Spencer, I admit, but even there they haven't got any of the strong grey wool socks I like to replace all the ones I've worn out since last week. Apart from that it's mostly museums as far as I can see. We did find one you'd have liked – a permanent outdoor exhibition of plumbing, all laid out so you can inspect the welds and everything. The sign says it's the Centre Pompidou, which isn't in Beth's pocket gem dictionary, but I've worked out it means Quiet Pumping Centre, and you certainly can't hear anything.

Back Saturday—
Charlie

NOEL PETTY

A Travel Agent's Confession

Do go and see Europe whatever you do;
We can send you by minibus, hearse, or canoe;
  It's a *sine qua non*
  With wading boots on
    To see Venice in spring,
    And our Tour's just the thing
To enjoy it before it's all gone.

They're not at all cliquey in Thessaloniki;
  They're frightfully sweet in Calais;
Though the Mafia maffick they're really seraphic
  In Sicily, *most* of the day.
  We can send you to curious coasts
    Where the law's not dictated by prudery,
  For we make a good rakeoff from people who take off
    Their pants on a beach that's for nudery.

Do you want to go French with the minimum fuss?
Or tackle the Alps from the back of a bus?
  Is your notion of peace
  Being Spartan in Greece?
    Behaving like toads
    On the island of Rhodes
Or not very nicely in Nice?

The average tourist, unless he's a purist,
  Can survive with bad food and worse bedding,
Which is why we can face recommending a place
  That we wouldn't ourselves be seen dead in.
  There are people – though where, never mind–
    It's not a great distance from Spain–
  Who pay us commission from your malnutrition;
    While for us – it's GREAT YARMOUTH again!

PAUL GRIFFIN

Torremolinos,
Sunday.

Been here three days and we're still trying to find the sea.
I think we were getting close yesterday, but we found
ourselves in between a US submarine crew and a Welsh
rugby club and had to cut back up a side street. We're
getting through a lot of Sangría, which is a kind of fruit
salad with wine in the cracks. We're still trying to work out
what you're supposed to do with the fruit. Must go now, May
wants to have another crack at finding the Med, just to say
she's seen it. Or was it the Adriatic? Anyway, as long as we
find one of them.

    Regards to Beth,
        Fred

Granada,
Tuesday.

Just here on a one-nighter from Torremolinos. Pedro on the coach says this is the place where they finally got rid of the moors, and it must have worked because there's certainly nothing but olive trees here now. Tomorrow they're taking us to the Alhambra, but they haven't told us what's showing yet. I hope it's in English.

Adios—
Fred

Seville,
Thursday.

A day trip this time. It wasn't supposed to be a mystery tour, but it's all mysterious to me. You know, Charlie, I don't understand this country. Down by the sea it's all bikinis and wet T-shirts, but up here where it's twice as hot they're all walking around in the streets in great black cloaks and hoods with a couple of holes for the eyes. I mean, I suppose it keeps the sun off but there must be better ways. I think there's a lot of house-moving going on too, because some of them (the blokes in black) are carting huge thrones and statues around on their shoulders. May says perhaps we came at a bad time. Still looking for the Med, by the way.

Home Saturday, in time for the snooker,
Fred

NOEL PETTY

You may prefer to go under your own steam. This will enable you to absorb more local colour on the way.

It seems very soon everyone'll
Be taking the train through the Chunnel
To go continental,
Though traffic through Kent'll
Be jammed up like sand in a funnel.

KATIE MALLETT

The ferry
Ain't merry;
The hover's
A bovver;
Flying
's too trying.

The tunnel, I hope,
will offer more scope.

D.A. PRINCE

What a Relief!

Underneath the waves you'll find me
On the way to France by train,
All me former fears behind me –
Tum no more seized up with pain.

Even standing in a station,
I can spend a penny when
Europe is me destination –
And uncross me legs again.

Vacuum-powered an' teflon-coated
Loos on chunnel trains have tanks.
To our comfort they're devoted
Now – for this relief, much thanks.

MARGARET ROGERS

Some Useful Continental Road Signs

France

Pierres Tombées:	Bistro ahead
Zone Bleu:	Red-light district
Virages sur 6km:	Feminist commune ahead

WFNWATSON

Poids Lourds:	Pilgrimage in progress
Priorité à Droite:	Go ahead, you're in the right
Bétteraves:	Go on, let your wife drive for a bit
Fin de Chantier:	No Singing Past This Point
Nids de Poules:	Caution: Poultry Nesting
Passage à Niveau:	New Road

Spain

Salida de Fabrica:	Light Lunches To Order
Autopista de Peaje:	Drunken Drivers Will Be Fined
Cruce Peligroso:	Religious Processions Ahead
Obras:	Topless Bathing Permitted

OBRAS
PROHIBIDO EL PASO

WFNwatson

Despacio:	Post Office
Centro Urbano:	School of Deportment

Germany

Ausfahrt:	Atmospheric Pollution
Ein Bahn:	EEC grain store

Kein Eingang:	Entry to pig farm
Links Fahren:	Sausage Lunches
Geschwindigkeit Verlangsamen:	By the Time You Have Finished Reading This Notice It May Already Be Too Late To Slow Down

Italy

Veicoli Lenti:	Car Hire
Solo Sorpasso:	Caution – Luciano Pavarotti ahead
Marcia Normale:	This is a probably a message to the Mayor from his mistress, and should be ignored
Transito con Pneumatico da Neve:	Inflatable military dinghies in transit

The Netherlands

Inhalen Verboden:	Toxic gas alert
Spoorwegovergang:	Snail crossing
Niet parkeren:	Mind your own business

Belgium

Schyf Verplicht:	You are in a Flemish-speaking area. Do not attempt O-level French beyond this point

NOEL PETTY

A Load of Boules

While driving through a small French village, I came upon a strange sight. On a piece of rough ground, a group of men were taking it in turn to toss large steel balls at a small white one. I stopped the car to watch and, seeing my puzzlement, one of the group approached me to ask, in very good English, if he could help.

'What are you doing?' I asked.

'That will take time to explain and it's a very hot day. Let's retire to somewhere more comfortable.'

He indicated an estaminet across the road. We trooped across, followed by his companions and a few villagers who were now taking an interest. I ordered a round of drinks for them all and settled down to hear my new-found friend's explanation.

'Have you not heard of the deadly Mediterranean Spitting Spider?'

I confessed my ignorance.

'Then you are very lucky. You English think there are no dangers in our countryside, but many fall victim to this creature every summer. We are Spitting Spider exterminators. They live in holes in the ground, rather like Trap-door Spiders and if an enemy approaches, they pop out and spit their venom as far as five metres, and then pop back in again. We are expert at finding their colonies, which we mark with a white ball.'

'I didn't notice any holes', I said.

'No, they are well disguised. That's why we need the white ball.'

'And I didn't see any spiders.'

'Good; now you realise the dangers – they are so quick!'

'But after you had aimed all your balls at the spiders, wasn't it dangerous to approach the colony, as I saw you do?'

'No, the impact of the balls frightens them and makes them hide in their holes for several minutes, so we have time to count the victims.'

'And how many victims have you caught today?'

'Only one.'

I had to be on my way so I thanked my informant and left them all to finish their drinks. As I departed, vowing to avoid the hidden risks of straying from the road, and if I did, to watch out for the little white balls, I heard the sound of distant laughter.

How good it was that these brave men found such pleasure in this public-spirited and dangerous pursuit.

ARTHUR P. COX

In the hills near the city of Parma,
You can camp in the field of a farma
Who is somewhat aloof –
But there's milk on the hoof,
And his wife is an absolute charma!

MICHAEL FOSTER

Bottoms Up!

One stormy night in Austria, near the Brenner Pass
A climber of our party fell down a deep crevasse.
We watched him go with horror, and shed a silent tear.
It really spoilt our evening; he was carrying the beer.

FRANK RICHARDS

How We Brought The Camping Gear
From Ghent To Aix

I sprang to the tent-flap, and Doris, and Bea;
I gargled, Bea gargled, we gargled all three.
'Are we there?' cried the twins as we folded the tent,
'No we're not,' I replied. 'We're at some place called
  Ghent,
And the sooner you're dressed we can all be away
To the place where we're aiming to be, which is Aix.

We'd arrived on the six o'clock ferry, you see,
My missus, the twins, Auntie Doris and me,
Intending to camp by the end of that day
At a camp site we'd heard about just outside Aix,
But the darkness came on, so our first night was spent
In a rather damp turnip-field somewhere near Ghent.

We asked at the tourist place which way to go.
'To Aix?' said the lady. 'I'm sure I don't know,
But set off for Paris, that's always the best,
And then when you're round it I think I'd suggest
You follow the Autoroute signs to Marseille
Then turn left at Lyons and ask there for Aix.'

We set off at once in the bright morning air
The twins calling every few miles, 'Are we there?'
With Auntie D. prodding me: 'Keep on the right!',
I motored all day and I motored all night
Till, just as the lady had told us it should,
At length into Aix the car shuddered and stood.

We asked at the tourist place where was the camp,
While poor Auntie Doris recovered from cramp,
But the gentleman said, in his frenchified twang,
'Non, non! Quel dommage! C'est ici Aix-les-Bains.
I'm sure what vous cherchez is Aix-en-Provence.
Nous fermerons now, so bon soir et bonne chance!'

'Which way do we go, though?' 'Vous turn round,'
  he said,
'Retournez a Lyons, then make pour le Med,

Go straight sur le main Autoroute du Soleil,
And that should deposit vous plumb into Aix.'
We drove through the night again, ragged and worn,
And entered our second Aix just before dawn.

As soon as the tourist place opened at ten,
We asked for the Camping all over again.
I saw by his face that the prospect was bleak:
'Hélas! Je regrette that the place that you seek'
– I saw Bea and Doris get ready to scream –
'Is the Island of Aix in Charente-Maritime.'

'Go back up the Autoroute – ne pas despair –
You'll soon find the great Autoroute des Deux Mers.
Just follow the signs to Toulouse and Bordeaux,
Then ask at Niort for the best way to go.
The place that you seek is a little remote,
But find La Rochelle and you'll soon get a boat.'

'Are we there?' cried the twins. 'No, not quite,' I replied,
As I bundled them up with Aunt Doris inside.
I could see that the axis of Doris and Bea
Was starting to blame the whole journey on me.
I got it all day and then all night as well
Till we saw the Atlantic and hit La Rochelle.

We asked, when the tourist place opened next day,
If our campsite was there, on the Island of Aix.
I could feel Auntie Doris's breath on my neck
As he flicked through his Carnets des Campings to check.
'Monsieur, I'm afraid – are you feeling unwell? –
The Aix that you want must be Aix-la-Chapelle.'

'You'd better go North East to Paris, that's clear,
It's always the best way to start out from here.
Then North on the Autoroute, turn right at Ghent'
– I coughed at this point to put Bea off the scent –
'Then left round Liège, the map's quite explicit,
And roll into Aix, you can't possibly miss it.'

I sprang to the saddle and started the car.
'He's told me the way and it doesn't sound far.'

But we drove through the night without sign of our goal,
And through the next day, paying toll after toll,
Till, just as the second day started to darken,
We stopped by a notice: WILLKOMMEN IN AACHEN.

'That's enough!' said Aunt Doris, and started to weep.
'That's it!' muttered Bea, and turned over to sleep.
'Is this it?' cried the twins. 'Is this it? Are we there?'
'No, we're not,' I replied, and was starting to swear
When I looked at the notice and gave a great yell:
'Look – Aachen – see – formerly Aix-la-Chapelle!'

We asked at the tourist place. 'Yes, that's the site,
Just park over there by the tree on the right.'
'Are we there?' cried the twins. 'Yes, we are,' I said,
   'Yes,'
'Let's run up the tent,' I said, flushed with success.
Then paused. 'Better not. It'll make too much work:
First thing in the morning we sail from Dunkirk.'

                                                    NOEL PETTY

Continental hotels have the usual range of facilities.

No Finn
Will scauna
Sauna
Unless
He lacks Finnesse . . .

                                        MICHAEL FOSTER

Protest to Continental Hoteliers

I am an ancient traveller
Who stoppeth at your inn
Where hot & cold awaiteth
But I'll not come again.
For there are no plugs
In your marble baths
To keep the WATER in!

ARDA LACEY

Helpful Notes From A Greek Hotel

1. Peoples of all manners use this hotel. You are welcome to it.
2. Guests are beseeched to empty chambers before midday, as new arrivers wish to fill them.
3. Before to possess guests for yourself in the Restaurant, to kindly obtain adhesion of the Receptionist.
4. If you wish to make a party in our rooms, the Manageress will make herself agreeable.
5. Our shop is open to show you things Greek people do except on Mondays.
6. Not to keep your valuables, but to give them away to the Manageress.

PAUL GRIFFIN

The Lorelei Rock Hotel

The River Rhine is a very popular and picturesque, – though uphill – route to Southern Germany, with many good hotels on the way. For attraction, none can compare with the legendary Lorelei Rock. A centuries old castle (or Schloss to the locals), it is situated high above a bend in the river.

Hidden by immense cliffs, the hotel would be difficult to locate were it not for its singing group, who spend all day performing at the water's edge. Calling themselves 'The Sirens', they are readily audible from several kilometres and their particular style called 'Rhine whine', like bagpipes, is better heard at a distance. At close range, though, they change to greetings of: 'Hello Sailor!'

There is always space for your boat, however big. The novel introduction of underwater moorings gives the nautical equivalent of a multi-storey car park. The age of some of the boats in the lower strata indicates the popularity of the hotel as a retirement home.

The Lorelei Rock Hotel is one of the chain, employing only female staff, operated by Valkyrie Hotels Ltd. Our correspondent was uncertain about their duties, which seemed to include all-night room service, but was pleased to note that the chambermaids had dispensed with the apron and coal-scuttle uniform of the parent hotel in Bavaria.

Among the many amenities are two wells, appropriately known as A and B. In keeping with their wish to cater for all tastes, the management have not overlooked the requirements of teetotallers, so the A-well (A, of course, standing for 'abstainer') contains water flowing in from the river. This appeals more to the connoisseur than the purist, for it has a characteristic and unforgettable flavour. The B-well supplies beer, and is a great attraction during the spring *bierfest* when the guests can become, as they say, B-well *schlossed*.

Your correspondent found only one general complaint about the Lorelei Rock Hotel. Every guest said that his bed was damp.

ARTHUR P. COX

Sightseeing should be high on your agenda; information for tourists is freely available.

Chaton-Sur-Mer
Michelin Map 51 4 – Pop. 1069

Set amid flat, marshy terrain a short distance from the Belgian border, Chaton is no longer 'sur mer'. Mostly devoted now to the assembly of light electrical components, it was completely razed in both World Wars. As a result, its architecture is unusually homogeneous. The main square features the low, angular buildings in grey cement typical of the rapid rebuilding programme of the late 1940s. The drain-grids, spared by repeated bombardments, are unusually bare and plain in a style popular under the Third Republic. In the town hall may be seen a signed photograph of Clement Attlee.

Church – Funds for the new Protestant church (1951) included a donation from the mayor and corporation of Watford. In gratitude, the head of a stag was carved by the local sculptor Guillaume Carbonade and placed in the porch. One of its antlers was damaged in a gale in 1960.

Mont du Diable – At the southern end of the town, this hill rears 20m over the surrounding countryside. In clear weather, the vista from its summit includes the Belgian villages of Houtem and Laisele.

Pan Museum – *Open from 10 a.m. to noon and 3 to 4 p.m. June-October, admission: 10F.*
The museum, housed in a former bicycle shop, holds a collection of almost forty pans of the flat, circular type used for making *crêpes*. Some are of local origin, the remainder gathered from a variety of sources in north-eastern France. To the left of the shop entrance used to be an enamel Peugeot sign: traces of the screw holes are still clearly visible.

Vallée de la Boue – *5km/3 miles to the west. Leave Chaton by the D55. At the Beaux Jours garden centre turn left on to an unmetalled road. Park by the EDF sub-station. 8 minutes walk to river.*

Now largely dry thanks to the area's irrigation needs, the Boue was once a vital waterway, giving access by boat to the Canal de la Basse Colme. It is now an important wildlife habitat. Newts regularly breed there and it is used by the Société Ornithologique de Chaton. There is a legend that those who cross the footbridge barefoot will enjoy happiness and good fortune.

BASIL RANSOME-DAVIES

A Returning Tourist Explains Greek Architecture

I'm pretty sure this is right, because I wrote it all down here, straight from the mouth of the guide who showed us round.

Greek architecture happens (usually) in ruins on top of pretty bumpy little hills where the coaches won't take you. A cropperless is what they call most of these hills, which is obviously a joke, because falling over is exactly what you can expect to do, either over stones on the track or over the solid mass of tourists who are on the way down while you are on the way up, or vice versa.

More often than not these ruins are temples, consisting of rows of pillars and not much more, and apparently it's terribly important to get the kind of pillars right. I think it's something like this:

1. Euphoric – zooms straight up into the air and is then severely flattened.

2. Tonic – rises rapidly to the top and then fizzes over the edges.

3. Cornucopian – stuffed solid all the way up and then bursts
    into fruity bits.

A name which makes rather more sense is a carryalid, which
is a pillar in the shape of a woman with a flat bit on top.

Then there are sometimes bits above these pillars with
carvings and so on: the artystage supports this artistic bit,
which is jestingly known as the squeeze because of the crush
of indistinguishable figures with bits broken off here and
there. A largish bit chopped out of an old wreck in Athens
is known as the Bulgin' Baubles and can now be seen in the
British Museum. Some of these temples have a sort of triangle
above all this – it's called the impediment, as it stops the
building going up any further – quite a good idea, really.

There's seldom anything of interest or indeed anything at
all inside these buildings, except tourists, but sometimes you
find a bit in the middle with a few extra pillars which, though
it doesn't look like one, is called the cellar. The Greeks liked
to see their gods (or perhaps their priests) well supplied with
booze and this was the most sacred bit of the temple.

That's the essence of it, anyway.

MARY HOLTBY

Some Practical Hints for Streetwise Tourists

Italy

Each church provides candles for an impromptu barbecue.

Custodians in Italian churches will occasionally challenge the dress of lady visitors. The correct response is to remove the offending garment and place it as an 'offering' before the nearest statue.

JOHN SWEETMAN

Germany

The German people welcome donations, however small, towards the rebuilding of the recently destroyed Berlin Wall.

D.A. PRINCE

Belgium

Don't forget to take the family for a nice bedtime drink in old dockside Antwerp, where the coffee shops are all clearly marked and the friendly waitresses sit in the windows to welcome you.

YVONNE REID

If you find one of the roadside lacemaker's cushions unattended, this is an invitation to try your skill. See if you can take the pattern a bit further!

NOEL PETTY

France

Every block of flats maintains its own prostitute in a flat beside the main entrance.

D.A. PRINCE

If the wine-waiter asks you to taste the wine, it is correct to spit it out. You then ask him to pour with the word 'Merde', a truncation of 'Maitre d'.'

NOEL PETTY

The Netherlands

All bicycles are state-owned, and free for the use of everyone.

NOEL PETTY

Britain

The Queen entertains paying guests to afternoon tea on Saturdays. To make a booking, slip a £20 note into the fist of the guardsman on duty outside Buckingham Palace.

Any London taxi-driver will be happy to advise on alternative bus routes.

D.A. PRINCE

Spain

The deck-chair attendants can be identified by their odd patent-leather hats. Ask one to set you up a chair – the service is free.

When entering the Spanish customs area from France, you may sell your surplus francs by calling out *'Viva Franco!'* This will ensure you instant attention.

NOEL PETTY

Your Questions Answered

Q. *Where would you advise travellers to go if they want to see the really important sights?*

Take the train first to **Lille**, where they manufacture the unmentionables, and then on to make **Aix** while the sun shines. Then travel south to **Avignon**, to sail in the famous punt, before crossing the Pyrenees and aiming for **Castile**, where they make the soap. Drop in at the tuneful town of **Guantanamera** on the way. Then it's off to **Faro**, which was the cradle of Egyptian civilisation, believe it or not, and up to **Gama**, where Vasco came from. Cross Spain and Portugal from your list!

Sur le Punt d'Avignon . . .

Fly across the Med to Italy, where a trip to **Bologna** will show you how to make that fabulous thick sauce, and a walk along the **Sabine mountains** will thrill you with its notorious local crop, rapeseed. I always go to **Ferrara**, where the racing cars are built; and no Italian trip is a complete without looking in on **Umbria**, where umbrage is cooked. Now on to Greece.

Greece is full of history: **Sparta, Olympia, Corinth, Necropolis, Drama, Peninsula, Roussos, Athos, Porthos** and **Aramis** all await you. The islands are delightful: my favourite is **Patmos**, named after a racing driver (**Stirlimos**, another so-named, is close by). Drink the **raki**, the **saki**, the **khaki**, and visit the tombs of Byron, Rupert Brooke and Keats, who is buried in an urn.

I hold no candle for Germany, but you must visit the power station in **Mainz**, and visit the HQ of the Scouting organisation in **Baden-Powell**. You could visit **Schleswig-Holstein** and try to answer the famous Question there, I suppose, but only on the way to Denmark, where the apples of **Zuider** are tasty, and the family spirit is alive in **Aarhuus** ('our house').

Now, down to Luxembourg, where there are far too many impressive places to list here, and then on, on to Belgium, where I recommend the port of **Liège** (where the princes came from, as in 'My Liege') and its 'ostend', or East End, where the Belgian Cockneys live. Holland next, and **Rotterdam, Amsterdam, Blastandam** and all the other sea-defences will ensure a 'dam' good time.

Scurry quickly to Ireland, go the long, long way to **Tipperary** (the road is frightful), visit the flutes in **Galway**, and sample the cooking in **Ovens**, near Cork. Then home to Great, Great Britain.

Q. What sports are popular in Europe?
Well, funnily enough, darts is very popular all over Europe, although the French have a quick version of it called ***vingt et un***. The French and Belgians play a game called ***boules***. All over both countries you can find the locals carrying their characteristically colourful set of plastic balls, which they throw in sandpits, or on a beach if they've got one. The Italians love guessing games, and there is a party special, popular with children, in which special *ravioli* is passed round

and nibbled, the winner being the one who guesses the contents correctly. It's called **pasta parcel**. But really, they play all the same sports as we do – cricket, snooker, Aunt Sally, Rugby League.

Q. What about bullfighting?
This is a very sensitive issue. As you know, the Spanish like to watch swordsmen (*pointilista*) waving a red cape (*flamenco*) at a bull (*pamplona*). When Spain joined the Market, this had to be kept off the agenda – a little unfair, since we had to give up hare-coursing, fish-baiting, pig-sticking and many other ancient English pastimes when we joined. A shocking film was circulated in Spain to dissuade the Spanish from continuing their dreadful hobby. It starred Sir Thomas Steele, and was entitled *Thomas the Toreador* (a *toreador* is the title of a man who cuts off the bull's ears). Unfortunately, the Spanish are a very musical nation, and there was a slightly catchy song in the film – all about cruelty – called *Uno pamplona blanca*, which went straight to the top of their hit parade. Nor does it help that writers like Ernest Fitzgerald, who wrote *For Whom the Bull Toils*, wrote about the killing so enthusiastically.

Q. Where can you ski?
Yoghurt.

BILL GREENWELL

← JOHN O'GROATS   93

EUROSEX

This is a topic which few guide books deal with at all adequately. We believe that in 1992, the time for coyness is past. The following pages indicate something of the rich variety of practices to be found in Europe.

A tumescent young man from Gerona
Had a long and extraordinary boner.
I have met those who say
That it reached all the way
To the Plaza Real, Barcelona.

A couple residing in Dreux
Grew bored with coition *chez eux,*
So they fucked on the floor
Of the café next door:
Évidemment, folie à deux.

In Munich the Man of the Year
Will have drunk twenty litres of beer,
Sung a military song,
Farted loudly and long,
And molested young girls from the rear.

In Sweden the way to have sex
Is to interface stomachs and necks
While contriving to look
At a medical book
For the right sets of muscles to flex.

There was a young blood of Turin
Whose penis was frightfully thin,
And when placed inside
His attractive young bride
Felt less like a prick than a pin.

Though their diet is Gouda and ham,
The Dutch practise sex from the pram.
They enjoy it so much,
Those inscrutable Dutch.
Yeah – play it again, Amsterdam.

A chef and a waitress in Nîmes
Struck up a *liaison intime*
She enjoyed *soixante-neuf*,
For the chef's *langue de boeuf*
Was renowned from Cap Ferrat to Rheims.

An athletic *señora* from Ronda
Once fellated her mate on his Honda.
It was oh-so-sublime
That he urged 'One more time!'
But to do it again was beyond her.

There's a rumour that men in Toulouse
Have a thingamajig about shoes,
And I hear that the brogue
Is enjoying a vogue –
It's the wing-tips that make them enthuse.

A shipyard apprentice from Bremen
(A city world-famous for he-men),
Incautiously busting
His condom by thrusting,
Submerged his fiancée in semen.

In the better-off suburbs of Bruges
The men are not built at all huge,
Which accounts for the wives
Leading lesbian lives
In their sable and diamonds and rouge.

BASIL RANSOME-DAVIES

EUROCUISINE

Good food and drink is at the root of Continental European Culture, and it is important for the would-be European to acquaint himself with its main features.

Do it yourself: A Bluffer's Guide to Euro-Gastronomy

From 1992 onwards we will, in the interests of international co-operation and profit, ceaselessly entertain European visitors in our homes.

So what do we serve them? The patriotic answer might be 'ordinary British food', but the poor sods probably get most of their meals from MacDonalds as it is. Perhaps it would be best to make the foreigner feel at home. The conscientious host will therefore mug up a few basic ethnic menus. This is simple and cheap and, since showing willing is an effective form of blackmail, will repay many times over such little trouble and ingenuity as is required.

Basic ingredients (suitable for all EuroCuisine):

1. Last week's loaf with the mould scraped off.

2. The collection of dried herbs in little jars someone gave you as a wedding present.

3. The stock cubes you bought after your last visit to Italy – when was it?

4. An onion.

5. A head of garlic.

6. Bottles of your favourite wines from each country. Drink
    the wine yourself, then make your own refills using a kit
    from your neighbourhood chemist. If you do not draw
    the corks in the presence of your guests it might almost
    be argued that no actual deception is involved in this
    practice. DO NOT use white wine bottles from Austria
    since everyone will assume they have been topped up
    with anti-freeze. The fact that this has not been done for
    some years makes no difference: food fads die hard.

Alternatively, you can fight back with our own regional
esoterica.

The essence of Scottish Cuisine is that familiar ingredients
(handfuls of oatmeal aside) turn up under exotic names. A
checklist is appended.

Howtowdie with Drappit Eggs:	Roast Chicken with Poached Eggs
Forfar Bridies:	Steak and Suet Pies
Inky Dinky:	Cold Beef with carrots, warmed in gravy
Clapshot:	Mashed Potatoes and Parsnips
Colcannon:	Sophisticated Bubble and Squeak
Kailkenny:	Creamy Bubble and Squeak
Rumbledethumps:	Bubble and Squeak with Chives
Skirlie:	Fried Onion with Oatmeal
Cloutie Dumpling:	Fruit Dumpling cooked in a Cloth

TOM AITKEN

French Wines

Dear Sir, as requested,
  I've carefully tested
The wine-growing systems of France;
  I've been in the cellars
  With numerous fellers
And left not a vintage to chance;
  For I've tasted chateaux
  From all parts of Bordeaux
And quartered the Burgundy fields;
  I've staggered through oceans
  Of talk with negociants
On corking and cuvées and yields.
  Of grapes, the Merlot,
  Chardonnay and Pinot,
The Cabernet, Syrah, Gamay,
  Are all in a mess
  In my mind, and to guess
Which is which I can't possibly say.
  But leave me alone
  With a Beaune, or a Rhône,
And I promise it won't go to waste;
  You can tell me it's classy,
  Or lengthy, or grassy,
  That it's pétillant, placid,
  Good-tempered, or acid;
  You can say that it's oaky,
  Or spicy, or smoky,
  Or a bit of a brute
  With masses of fruit,
But the truth is, I just like the taste.

PAUL GRIFFIN

Croissantry . . .

The croissant is defined as a flaky, crescent-shaped bread roll made of a yeast dough similar to puff pastry, and it is the staple form of the Continental so-called breakfast in France. The same alleged meal, which scarcely dents, let alone breaks, the fast of the Britisher who normally requires cereal, eggs, bacon, toast and marmalade to perform that function, may, in other European countries, consist instead of cake or biscuits, even, in Holland, of bread and cheese. But definitely in France, you pays your money and you takes your croissant.

It is sometimes seen to be eaten dry, especially by young women hurrying to work and breakfasting as they go along. By more leisured classes or earlier risers it is taken at table, buttered, jammed, honeyed or whatever. But the method most commonly seen of a morning in the restaurant is by 'dunking' (from the town of Dunkerque, or vice versa). The croissant is held by one curved end or horn, while the other is 'dunked' (gently dipped) into the outsize French breakfast-cup of *café-au-lait*. In non-French hotels, where cups are smaller, a cereal-bowl is often used, both for drinking from and for dunking in. '*Après-dunke*', with an adroit twist of the wrist in a clockwise or off-break direction, the soggy portion is brought up to engage with a sharp downward snap of the teeth. The importance of speed, timing and accuracy in this manoeuvre cannot be overemphasised: too long in the liquid and the dunked end becomes so coffee-logged that disintegration sets in, so that on being raised it belly-flops obscenely and messily back into the cup. The same occurs if the off-break is performed too slowly; while if too fast or with poor control, the inept croissantier or his neighbours, may well receive a full toss in the eye.

Despite intensive research, it is not possible to establish a reason for the French preference for this meagre breakfast or petty day-journey as they rightly term it. It is assumed to be possibly in the interest of either economy or time-saving, vide street consumption described above; or perhaps to permit semi-starvation by noon to be advanced as a credible excuse for the normal French luncheon interval of three or four hours, comprising a solid and leisurely repast plus time to spare for a couple of hours chez the chère amie. Whatever the reason, it certainly does not seem to be personal taste or lack of appetite, judging by the whole-hearted way in which Gallic guests in international hotels are seen at the buffet to undergo an enthusiastic, instant road-to-Damascus

Obscene belly-flop back into the cup

conversion to a grande alliance of 'English breakfast' of bacon, eggs and tomato; German *frühstuck* of *schinkenwurst*, rolls, butter, fruit and cereal, and Dutch *ontbijt* of breads, cheeses, cakes and cold ham. It is not known whether on returning to La Patrie they revert to frugal croissantry or continue to breakfast *à la Perfide Anglais*.

W.F.N. WATSON

. . . *And Other Breakfasts*

Some years ago I discovered the French Railways English breakfast. It was served in the cooking pan – anything else would have been impossible. You cover the bottom of the pan with rashers of bacon and break two eggs on them. The bacon is then fried until done, leaving the eggs almost uncooked, a result which cannot be obtained in any other way.

A technique from the Balkans which has taken many years of development, perhaps since the days of Homer, is Greek Toast. You find a large flat rock and at daybreak, cover it with slices of bread. At midday you turn over those which have not curled up enough to roll into the bushes and the final slightly sun-burned results are collected up at sunset to be served for breakfast the next day. The wild birds do not eat the toast first because it is far too hard for their beaks. Note how many species of the region have bent ones. This is solely due to Greek Toast.

ARTHUR P. COX

Claret

Chateau Talbot, Chateau Palmer, Chateaux Canon and
    Belair,
    Not to speak of Chateau Margaux, great Latour, Gruaud-
      Larose,
Lovely names for lovely liquor, purple, secretive and
    spare,
    Vapourizing on the palate, leaving scents and afterglows.

Rich and ripe they leave St Julien, St Emilion, Haut-
    Médoc,
    Travel out to spread their riches even to the dullish
      Brits;
Hard-faced dealers pay the needful, fill their cellars, turn
    the lock –

This is something called investment, making people lose
their wits.

Lost in cellars till the market soars to prices few can pay,
Decent claret is for no one till its price is out of reach.
Here's a glass. A tenner for it? Now I know why people
say:
'Bring the plonk out, Uncle Raymond, let's go picnic
on the beach!'

PAUL GRIFFIN

Let's Not Halt Awhile

More than anywhere else, France is a country in which you
may take pot luck in restaurants with reasonable confidence.
However, there are exceptions – and not only those places
that have loud signs in English, attract plenty of Americans
or specialise in *nouvelle cuisine*. Here is a generic guide to the
less than truly wonderful.

The Past Glories

It will be an attractive building, often ivy-clad, with a name
like *La Chope d'Or* or *L'Hostellerie du Roi*. The menu is designed
to resemble a parchment scroll, and is very extensive. There is
a superabundance of waiting staff crisply dressed, sporting
an aloof professional air. The deficiencies are in the kitchen,
however. You will be urged to sample the *menu gastronomique*,
twice the price of the standard *prix fixe*. All its most interesting dishes carry heavy supplements. Wine probably starts at
80 francs at bottle; for this you will not get much more than a
vin de table. Also, the menu is deceptively long. Mostly, it is
different sauces. These are floury, and spooned on in thick
dollops they disguise the questionable quality of the meat or
fish. The delight expressed by the manager when you pay
the bill is from the heart.

The Fresh Start.

This out-of-the-way hotel-restaurant is going places, or so the madman who owns it has decided. His non-stop talk is peppered with the word *dynamisme*. Try to address him in French and he will assume you are German and tell you of the time he worked in Trier. He is prone to bursts of song as he races about with a rattling tray. He offers snacks, including a sort of ploughman's lunch, the *assiette randonneur*, and a few easy-cook hot dishes. He has arranged pony rides for the kids. He rents out bicycles. In the evening he plays English pop music and barbecues *merguez*. Having bought a run-down joint at a knock-down price, he is applying the entrepreneurial *dynamisme* which he is convinced France, and especially the Midi, needs. He knows everything and does everything except leave his customers alone.

The Third Age

Gentlepersons *en retraite* flock here for the bland, watery food which they trust not to disturb their fragile digestive systems. The dining room is faded, without colour. Even the staff seem anaemic. You feel sinful ordering wine, because no one else is drinking it. Instead, the grey, elderly people who only communicate in nods and brief murmurs will be drinking mineral water. There is a bottle on each table, though not one will get finished. The faint, tinkling noise in the background is Richard Clayderman, an endless loop of him. In the lobby sits a pile of out-of-date retirement magazines, each packed with advertisements for specialised cures at spa towns. You begin to hope that no one will actually die *in situ*, and feel relief when their cars roar away like fighter planes. The atmosphere of painstaking, low-key politeness, is a strain, and when you go, you still feel slightly hungry.

The Take It Or Leave It

Nothing wrong with the food here – when you get it. The restaurant seems warm and welcoming, and the menu looks good and well-priced. The problem which you cannot realise until it is too late, is that the small family who run the place are all drunk and engaged in a deep quarrel with one another. The daughter does not want to wait table. She wants to be at the movies with her boyfriend, and her attitude lets you know it. The father tears frenziedly between kitchen and dining room, shouting unintelligibly. The mother is getting defiantly pissed at the bar and flirting with anyone who calls in for a casual Pernod. Intimidated by all the mysterious passion, you put up, helplessly, with the wayward service. You may get away by eleven if you're lucky. If you're even luckier, the bill will have been miscalculated in your favour. It may just be worth it if you're in a mood of humorous detachment.

BASIL RANSOME-DAVIES

A Report on Spaghetting

Mastery of the mysteries of Spaghetti Function was observed to be of a generally low standard and haphazard in approach. Four main methods were noted, as detailed below.

a) *Britischer*s and Germans, after fairly ineffectual efforts to cut up the spaghetti, then forked or spooned it into the mouth, which left numerous untidily trailing ends. These were then sucked up to rendez-vous with the rest of the mouthful, invariably leaving one long and refractory tube to be either hooked out with fork or finger, or drawn up into the mouth like an anchor-chain disappearing into the cat's-eye, or a serpent into a drain. The Britische approach, it should be added, often began with a forlorn attempt to deal with this arcane substance as though with a macaroni pudding.

b) The *Méthode Française* was via the Baden Bend, without preliminary chopping, which looked not like one disappearing snake but an entire reptile family, and noisily hissing.

c)   An alleged mode recalled by one committee person, of the trailing ends being trimmed off with scissors at lip-level by the spaghetteer or by a waiter, was traced to a film of the late M. Charlot Chaplin, and was not observed in practice.

d)   The Britkinder method was similar to b) above, with spoon, fork, knife and fingers employed even more untidily.

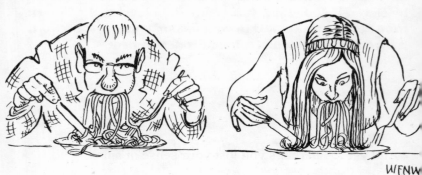

Spaghetting   Jugged Hair

e)   The Italian Connection involved the holding of the spoon in the left hand, while the fork in the right was plunged into the tangled skein. This, supported by the spoon also, was raised and lowered a distance of some 20 cms several times to free it from the main jumble, after which the fork, pressed into the bowl of the spoon, was remorselessly rotated to wind the skein on to the fork in an oval ball as of knitting wool. This was then inserted into the mouth leaving seldom more than one short, disconsolate end to be vacuumed à bord. This adroit process was then repeated until the whole was consumed.

The recommendation of the Committee is that spaghetting be avoided by those non-Italians who are not virtuosi of the Italian Connection.

W.F.N. WATSON

A Fragrant Libel

You wrote of Burgundy when it was Claret!
　What other libel can compare to this?
What Queensberry wrote of Wilde? What Mr Barrett
　Wrote of Elizabeth when he came to miss
　　His erring daughter?
　　　If you should come to dine
　　　You'll not again have wine;
　　I'll give you water.
And yet . . . perhaps you lost your sense of smell,
　And I'm uncharitable. Even so,
You must have been without your taste as well:
　It's rare for all one's faculties to go
　　At one fell swoop.
　　　Besides, as I recall,
　　　You found the wherewithal
　　To praise the soup.
No, it's quite clear the best that you deserve
　Is burgers, chips, and shandy in a garret;
For you insulted France, and had the nerve
　To write of Burgundy when it was Claret.

PAUL GRIFFIN

Diary Of A Wine Writer

The following is an unedited extract from the diary of a well-known wine-writer on a tasting trip to the Bordeaux region.

Monday

Woke at 6. Marvellous morning, delicious air, soft and perfumed. Jogged twice round the parc and had a quick dip before breakfast. Declined coffee despite delicious aroma. Must keep taste buds fresh. Toured Pauillac in a.m., then lunch and more tastings at St Julien. Some of the early '80s wonderfully delicate and fragrant now, and the '84s and '85s really come out to meet you.

After dinner a lecture with tastings by an organic chemist on the complexities of Bordeaux. Concluded human palate a much more subtle instrument than his spectrometers. Absolutely fascinating, though; stayed up till midnight discussing conclusions over some interesting Mouton Rothschilds.

Tuesday

Got up at 8, decided give jog a miss. Toured Margaux in a.m. with more tastings before lunch. Thought flavours a bit less sharply defined than yesterday; still, lovely stuff. In p.m. a lecture on conjectural reconstruction of pre-phylloxera taste of Bordeaux, with examples to taste. Room rather warm, fell asleep. Woke in time for tasting, though.

Wednesday

Rose at 10, just caught breakfast but couldn't manage much. Went on visit to caves north of river, St Emilion or something. Tasted some big-nosed stuff that went down jolly well, but didn't quite catch name. Cut lecture after dinner, had 2/3 brandies and went to bed.

Thursday

Slept till noon nearly. Light extraordinarily bright today. Had to wear dark glasses to go down for lunch. Fell down last flight, destroying prized Sèvres vase in process. After lunch, tastings at St Estèphe. Great afternoon – can't beat the old vino I always say. Missed dinner, watched TV in bedroom. Couldn't understand a word but pictures restful.

Friday

Got down about two. Missed breakfast, missed lunch, and missed coach to Pomerol or somewhere. Spent afternoon in bar, having private tasting of Pernods. Feeling just a bit below par. Touch of the old malaria coming on, perhaps.

The diary ends here. Being incomplete, the notes are of limited value as a guide for wine-lovers, but do offer a fascinating insight into how connoisseurs of fine wines go about their work.

NOEL PETTY

One final word of warning: like us, the Continentals have their food scares.

Hard Cheese: New Loony Cow Euro-Shock

Rumours of a severe psychiatric disorder among French cattle are causing grave alarm throughout Europe.

British farmers, permanently angry after a series of clashes with the French, are calling for a complete ban on imports of beef and dairy products from France because of 'laughing cow disease'.

But while the French government stayed silent on the matter last night, the country's milk and meat producers denounced the British demand as 'hysterical'. One said: '*Nom d'un nom*! We believe it all started because some English fool noticed a picture of a laughing cow on a packet of French cheese.

'It is all ridiculous. Our cows do not laugh, any more than British farmers do.'

But a leading British cattle breeder declared: 'There is no doubt that laughing French cows are producing cheese which our children are eating. And youngsters have been seen laughing their heads off at school.'

'Putting two and two together, we advise mothers: stick to good old Cheddar for the kiddies' sake – at least until this scare ends and another one starts.'

The Ministry of Agriculture is taking the matter seriously. It is assembling a team of cow psychiatrists – 'not an easy job,' said a spokesman – to investigate selected herds in France.

A recent opinion poll indicated that few people were seriously worried about 'laughing cow disease'. Here are some comments:

A 70-year-old man: 'Cripes, if I was a bloody French cow, or a French farmer, I'd be laughing all the way to the bank.'

A 19-year-old girl student: 'I've heard they do awful things to make those cows laugh, like they feed up those poor geese for pâté.'

A 30-year-old lager drinker: 'I wouldn't have no part of a laughing cow, no more than I'd eat frog's legs, but it's a free continent, innit?'

PETER VEALE

Your Questions Answered

Q. What is the Common Agricultural Policy?

This is one of the main things that countries joining the Common Market have to agree to. Each country has to use every bit of its resources to be able to give something to its friends (rather like Christmas, when you come to think of it). That means using all the land to grow vegetables and crops – even land which is just sitting there doing nothing, like village commons for a start. The Common Agricultural Policy means we all agree to grow something on any land where it will grow. Dartmoor is expected to be a market garden by the year 2020. It will be known as 'Heath Heath' after the man who took us into Europe.

Q. I have often seen journalists writing about something known as a CAP. What exactly is a CAP?

Every country in the Common Market has to be stopped from growing too much food, otherwise it is just a waste (or the people living in the country get very fat indeed). For instance, they are very fond of goats' cheese in France – and, before the Common Market started up, they used to produce a ridiculous amount of it. They had to eat it for *petit déjeuner*, *grand déjeuner*, every *déjeuner* going. Now there is a CAP on goats' cheese and the French are healthier as a result. In the meantime, the goats have been given a new job. They are used to graze the grass from Commons, so that other crops can be sown. And they are also used for modelling for stories in children's books, an awful lot of which are about goats (*The Three Billygoats Gruff*, *The Lonely Goatherd*, *Goat Ellut On The Mountain*, *The Goat Of Many Colours* and so on).

Q. What is a Dutch CAP?

This is a special policy applied to Holland, where tulips are allowed to be grown in their millions – far more than are needed. Partly this is to disguise the really rather dull Dutch landscape. Some of the tulips are picked to make the famous Sauce Hollandaise.

Q. *What is the Butter Mountain?*

Let us first clear up the silly idea that it is a mountain, like the Alp, made out of butter. No-one has ever taken ropes, axes, picks and croutons and tried to climb it! It is in fact a Health Precaution. Too much butter is bad for you. But you cannot stop cows producing dairy goods – indeed, in some parts of Europe, even goats and sheep are known to produce dairy goods, something we have managed to prevent in this country. The sensible answer to this problem, therefore, has been to stockpile, in a giant freezer, all the extra butter left over after each country has been allowed its ration.

Q. *What happens to the Butter Mountain? What does it look like? What are its advantages?*

The Butter Mountain is arranged as a huge pyramid, and is kept in a large freezer which moves between Brussels and Strasbourg. It is constantly maintained by a team of butter-boys and -girls, who also act as guides to those who wish to inspect it. The Butter Mountain is very useful. It is used to feed starving Russians (who have no cows, and therefore no cheese, either). It is also very good insurance against serious outbreaks of Mad Cow Disease (*Bovrili Spinacchio Encefilato*, as the Italians call it), and also against War, when we would need to top up supplies. Furthermore, the Butter Mountain pays for itself by providing all Europe's airlines with pre-packed portions of butter – known as 'pats' after the Aer Lingus stewards who first introduced them. This cuts the cost of aviation very considerably.

Q. *What is the Wine Lake?*

This is a famous and enormous pool beneath Luxembourg, into which each Common Market country pours some of its best vino. The resulting blend is then bottled and sold (hence the legend 'made from the wines of different EEC countries'). Since Greece joined the Common Market, the addition of *retsina* (Greek for 'eye-opener') has made for a fascinating new flavour.

Eye-opener

Q. *Are there any other stockpiles?*
Yes. The Spaghetti Hoop, The Biscuit Barrel, The Hamburger Hill, The Pasta Collection, The Olive Ocean, The Rye Heap, The Maize Maze, and The Blood Banks are among the many reserve supplies upon which we may draw in times of crisis. My own favourite is the Sheep Dip, in which quantities of mutton are kept marinading in subtle blends of EEC spices.

Q. *Who are the major wine-makers, cider-farmers, distillers and brewers in Europe? Where would I go to drink the proper stuff?*
You can usually tell where a drink has come from by

looking at its name. For instance, there is a drink called VAT 69 which pretty obviously comes from The Vatican, vintage of 1969 (such an excellent year that we hardly ever hear of other harvests). **Sherry** sounds English, but is really French, being an anglicisation of 'Chérie', i.e. a very dear, or costly drink. It is made using water from the river Cher, which flows through the district of the same name. **Port** comes from Port Talbot in Wales, which is why it is often mixed with lemon, the Welsh national fruit. **Beer** was first made in Opladen, which is near Dusseldorf in Germany; **lager** is Spanish, and originates in the port of La Garrucha (the reason supplies are so plentiful to British holidaymakers); *Liebfrau* is not made from mothers' milk as is so often feared, but from that of cows. **Whisky?** Scotch whisky comes from Scotland; Irish whisky comes from Ireland; and Malt whisky comes from Malta. **Madeira** comes from Majorca. No-one's sure where **wine** was first made, but the likeliest places are Finland and Vinland (America – Vinland is what the Vikings called it).

Q. What about soft drinks?
That beautifully refreshing and fizzy orange drink **Tango** comes from the centre of Spain, where oranges are drunk, and roses are clenched between the teeth. There is a beautiful dance named after this popular beverage, in which the woman wears a praying *mantis*, or shawl, and *castanet* stockings. The man is called the *flamenco*, or flamingo, after the way he inclines his neck to the woman. In Crete, they dance the *hoki-koki*, and this too is a dance named after a drink – *koki*, or, as we know it, **Coke**. Eire is the source of **Sprite**, which is supposedly the drink of the leprechauns. And **Fanta** comes from Santa Cruz in Spain (where it is called Santa – our pronunciation comes from the funny way we used to write our 'S'). **Lemonade** is made in every village, town or city throughout Europe, although its strength varies. Most road signs or proper maps will give you the current

strength underneath the name (e.g. *pop* 14,534); Berlin's
is said to be particularly potent.

Q. Where does bottled water come from?
This is all made in Spa. – which is short for Spain. It was
in very short supply until Spain joined the EEC, which
is why it used to be so expensive. There is one brown
water supply which some people drink, but we do not
recommend it. This is taken straight from the River Tizer
in Rome, and is named after it.

Q. What is the European for 'Cheers!'?
A number of possibilities are being aired. In hotels,
people tend to call **Hasta la visa**!, but most locals
will soon greet you with **mana la mancha**, or (literally)
'Down the hatch'. Certainly, we would not recommend
the insufferably pretentious **Proust!**

Q. Is it true that the best ice-cream comes from Italy?
Funnily enough, it isn't. The French make the finest of
all the creamy delights in Europe. Legend has it that Joan
of Arc was caught in a snowstorm with a cow, its udder
bursting. Deftly she grasped the teats, and extracted the
hard buttery substance. When local people came to see
the miracle, they were overcome by its taste, and Lyons
Maid remains Europe's most popular brand.

Q. What is a baguette?
A baby bague. The French use it for shopping.

BILL GREENWELL

Joan . . . caught in a snowstorm with a cow.

EUROLOOS

The enquiring European should aim to be well-prepared for the variety of post-prandial arrangements likely to be encountered.

The pre-lunch *pastis* hit the spot.
The wine was insolent, robust.
The steak, bestrewn with parsley dust.
Was tasty, tender, rare and hot.
The *mousse au chocolat* a must.
The Calva apple-rich.

So time to light a cigarette
(The restaurant abounds with smoke)
And be a debonairish bloke?
A wishful thought: the food you ate
Has stirred things up, and it's no joke,
That frantic rectal itch.

Le water is across the yard.
Where Stella crates are stacked like bricks
And someone's dog morosely licks
Its testicles. The choice is hard,
Unlike your bowels. What a fix –
Yet still you hesitate.

Sure, hesitate, but not for long
Before you wrench aside the door:
Ceramic footsteps on the floor,
A string-pull flush, and what a pong,
Like dead whales rotting on the shore . . .
At least you're not too late.

You crouch above the evidence
Of other users of the hole
In darkness, with no toilet roll,
And half-relieved, although half-tense
In case some slip of palm or sole
Should land you in the *merde*.

Omitting details, this ordeal
Can be completed with success.
Yet why's the bog a noisome mess
When elegance adorned the meal?
I asked a man in Bourg-en-Bresse,
But bugger-all he cared

BASIL RANSOME-DAVIES

The Loos of Europe

The British have lots of views
on European loos.
They say the French ones are just holes in the ground –
it's immoral and very unsound.
But for Yugoslavian Ladies and Gents
you have to choose
between Ladies' and Gentlemen's shoes –
it's just a huge emblematic shoe
that holds out hope to stressful you!

GAVIN EWART

The Loocu – A Proposal

Now that we're all good Europeans, let's get our act together
regarding coins and sexist signs at public loos.
  Let's avoid confusion. Let's not be misled by the silhouette
in trousers. Many an absent-minded woman travels in slacks.

Conversely, Scots, Greek and Albanian males may prefer to travel in kilts.

If no sign exists, other than the letters WC, this means that all are welcome. Partings of the way are generally made plain in various European languages after entry. But be prepared for the unexpected.

Some loos are free. Some require coins. There is no knowing. Therefore, be prepared to carry a bag full of loose coins of various denominations.

Perhaps there is something to be said for a common coinage, such as the ECU; a LOOCU at a fixed rate and size throughout Europe would be even more useful. No one would need to know the language, but everyone would know exactly what it was for!

ARDA LACEY

Eurograffiti From European Loos

Montmartre
Girls who drink in France, just ponder –
Absinthe makes the heart grow fonder . . .

MICHAEL FOSTER

The Vatican
Contraception is the odium of the papal.

KATIE MALLETT

Marbella
Oh to be in England now that April's there;
I must look out my wellies and my thermal underwear!

FRANK RICHARDS

Dublin

Parnell
Fell,
After having it away
With Mrs O'Shea

RON RUBIN

Paris

Girls! Leave those French *gentilhommes* in no doubt
That they jolly well can't Messieurs about.

W.F.N. WATSON

Belfast

Roared Rev Ian Paisley
Crazily:
'God
Is a Prod!'

RON RUBIN

John O'Groats

O my luve's like a red, red rose
Especially about the nose,
For the braw bricht winds of Caledonia
Gave her pneumonia.

FIONA PITT KETHLEY

Florence

The Uffizi
Is not so ritzi
's a matter of fact, it's totally naff –
Hasn't even got a decent caff.

E.O. PARROTT

The British Museum

The Greeks had a word for it – theft.

STANLEY J. SHARPLESS

Strasbourg

'We must mind our P's and Ecus.'

STANLEY J. SHARPLESS

Clermont-Ferrand

Ladies met in bistros in Paris
Are not the sort you maris.

W.F.N. WATSON

Liverpool

If we don't build a high-speed link
To the Channel Tunnel,
What benefits will come our way?
    None'll.

STANLEY J. SHARPLESS

Hamburg

When you're chatting her up, a Fraülein
May adopt a rather caülein;
A Frau
Seems different, somehau.

W.F.N. WATSON

Brussels
    Oui, oui! It's that mannequin again!

                                                  PETER VEALE

London, Westminster Bridge
    Earth has not anything to show more fair;
    I cannot see a tourist anywhere.

                                             E.O. PARROTT

Stratford-on-Avon
    To be, or not to be; that is the question
    Unless you come up with a third suggestion.

                                           PETER VEALE

EUROSPEECH

The British are not traditionally well-versed in the languages of other nations. This need not be a cause for despair, however; a great deal can be achieved through phrase books, intelligent interpretation of foreign words and a willingness to compromise by both sides.

Let's Sprachen Deutschlisch

English Tourist: Diese ist certainlisch ein wunderbar Tafel-wein. Already ich quite gepissed feel.

German Host: Ja, ja! Wir sellen quite a lot von diese Wein zu die Englisch. Es ist 'Liebfraumilch' genommt.

E.T.: Liebfraumilch? Du kannst nicht be serious? In Deutsch-land man macht Wein von *milch*?

G.H.: (*sotto voce*) Wir haben ein richtig one hier. (*aloud*) Nein, nein, mein Herr. Das ist only ein Weinmetafor. Ein bisschen like 'Bullsblood', für example. Wein ist always von Grapen gemacht, natürlich.

E.T.: Nicht so, actuallisch. In England wir priden uns auf unsere Homemadeweinen. Man kann of course ein Grapenkonsenträt usen, like ein Bootsweinmäkingkit für example, aber ich prefer die Ingredienten von Natur – Elderberrywein, Mangelwurzelwein, Kompostwein . . .

G.H.: Mein Gott! Und was about der Realale? Man hat mir gesagt that Englischerbier von warm Washingupwasser gemacht ist, aber up till now ich believed it nicht!

E.T. (through clenched teeth) Ha, ha! Sehr droll! Auf secondthoughts, diese Wein ist nicht so gut . . .

PETER NORMAN

Torre Pendente, or Tour Hang-ups

'The administration declines all responsibility for possible accidents and will denounce the transgressors in case of damages.' Thus, unambiguously, in an 'archaeological area'; but outside, what of the potential transgressors who find themselves in a linguistic wilderness of mysterious signs, where grim admonitions compete with grotesque allurements, puzzling advertisements and perverse announcements?

No more 'care of painture', or 'Trieste is very choreographical and scenic': we are now faced with the real thing and have to tease out a meaning as we travel. *Rallentare!* we can readily interpret as 'Get a move on', and *Continua*, 'Keep it up! but look out – down there is a crazy road (*via dotto*), and here we are warned of hazardous weather conditions: a frosty area (*rimozone*) or very thick mist (*foggia grande*). We could try the mobile canteen (*mobil servizio*) where it's possible to choose your fish (*elletrauto*), but alas! this park is for classy German cars only (*supermercato*). It might be as well to avoid the conference of windbags (*confartigianato*), and not to be so bold as to enter the loos for lecturers only (DONNE) . . .

Yet it seems that on all sides, paradoxically, we are offered a unique sensation (*senso unico*), and this vague, if intriguing, promise occasionally becomes more specific in such regrettable notices as *Antico Trullo* (old woman of easy virtue) or *Campo Sportivo* (gay goings-on). Of course we are hardly qualified to do much about these when there is emphatically no currency exchange (*banchino intransitabile*) – which equally prevents us from laying out money on crummy junk (*grotte*), a self-playing violin (*autostrada*), or a puppy-basket (*porto dogana*). Anyway, a notice in the same area warns *Imbarco* (barking prohibited) – no doubt for fear of distracting the performers in 'One Man and his Dog' (*colle del sole*).

But madness is setting in – why the badtempered butler (*crossodomo*)? Is it he whose intransigence inspired the moving legend *Parcheggio / Lavaggio* (I'm dying of thirst and I need a wash)? By now we can identify with those characters described by a guide as 'desperated pipple'; so desperated, perhaps, that in order not to 'commit all sorts of things in contrast to the dignity and respect of the places' we should betake ourselves to the *terminal regionale* – that country from whose bourn no traveller returns . . .

MARY HOLTBY

Puppy basket . . . Barking prohibited

Pronunciation Mnemonics For Place Names

A rugger fanatic from Nîmes
Once scored twenty tries in a drîmes.
When he dived for one more
He woke up, on the floor –
Things are not always quite what they sîmes . . .

MICHAEL FOSTER

There was a young lady of Nantes
Who murmured: 'I know what you wantes.
  If you asked me I would,
  And I know that I could
Procure you the plumes of my tantes.'

E.O. PARROTT

The chap in the train at St Gotthard
Turned out to be rather a rotthard
He shocked all the Swiss
By starting to piss
And using their coats as a blotthard.

GINA BERKELEY

There once was a housewife of Pisa
Who carelessly fell in the freezer.
  It's not very nice
  When your spouse turns to ice,
And disposal's a bit of a teaser.

MARY HOLTBY

Notes On The Danish Tongue

There is only one fault to find with this delightful and
enlightened tribe who, after all, have the inestimable social

advantage of having settled half England in the 11th century and ruled the whole lot for almost thirty years. Thus they provided the monarchy-loving English with one nearly-king, Sweyn Forkbeard; one Supaking, Cnut the Water-Repellant, and two shockers, Harold Harebrain and Harthacnut, both right bastards, though legally only the former could be called a proper bastard. Stacks of Eurobritish place-names demonstrate our affinity with the Danskers, so that if the name of your neck of the woods ends in -by, -thorpe or -hulme you can claim that your forebears were Vikings. It is therefore painful to state that after their thus getting off to a head start, the one Great Danish fault aforementioned, and bar to greater understanding of their ways and traits, is the Gloomy Danish language.

Cnut the Water–Repellent

It is not just the matter of the sounds they utter when talking, unintelligible and unidentifiable though they are; it's the unreasonable and baffling impossibility of picking up a tiny working smattering of it from a phrase-book, as every earnest True–Brit traveller seeks to do in order to make contact and build relationships with the natives everywhere he goes. But not in Denmark. As an example, consider a conversation with a Danish friend who had kindly arranged a marvellous holiday for us at a delightful farm-cum-inn at the edge of the forest on a Danish island. But, he told us, they don't speak English. However, I remembered that the great traveller and linguist George Borrow reckoned he taught himself Danish simply by procuring a Danish Bible, so I organised the following Borrovian-style dialogue:

Myself: No problem. I've often had to manage with phrase-books and Grammars – German, Arabic, Urdu, Dutch, Italian – so could you lend me a Danish Grammar Book, or Dictionary?

Georg: What for?

Myself: So that I can speak to the people at the inn.

Georg: You cannot speak Danish from a book.

Myself: I'm sure I can manage enough to make our needs understood.

Georg: You cannot speak Danish from a book.

Myself: Well, have you a book, so that I can try?

Georg: I have a dictionary. Please keep it. But you cannot etc., etc.

He produces a book. It is entitled *Gyldenals rde Ordbger. Engelsk–Dansk*, and I have it beside me now as I write.

Myself: Thank you very much, Georg.

I flip the dictionary open at random. Page 114. Find a familiar word, 'Duck (subst.)', and I point to the Danish word, which is 'And'.

Myself: Now, this word; is it 'ah-nd' or 'and'?

Georg: It is 'eh-uh'.

[It seems that a Danish word either looks entirely familiar, like 'and', and sounds like nothing on earth, or looks utterly daunting, like 'børnehjælpsdag' and sounds oddly familiar – 'bairn-helps-dag', and means just that – Help the Children Day. But mostly, like 'tandlægevæsen sygeplejerske' (Dental Nurse, if you need one), it's as impossible as it looks; and I don't know about G. Borrow and his Bible, but I reckon Georg was nearer the mark; you cannot praje Dansk from a bog.]

W.F.N. WATSON

Vile as the pun, I dare to utter it –
That Yugoslavian tongues must all be split
How else could people speak or understand
The names of towns and islands in their land?

Porec, and Krk, Ljubljana and Lyubinje,
Grke, Hvar, Cenj, Skopje, and Trebinje,
Vrsac and Vrbas beat your tongue, I'll bet,
And so do Plevlja, Gracac, and Mljet.

Beyond Dubrovnik, Yugoslavia ends,
And black Albania unknown miles extends;
Then, where green Corfu lifts her northern peak,
Let tongues relax, for all the names are Greek.

PAUL GRIFFIN

Eating Out In Greece

The Greeks' ancestors taught us to be free,
With every town its own democracy;
Now their descendants hear the song they sang
And, feeling free, let all the rest go hang.
One Greek, one point of view, entire, unique;
Were two identical, they'd not be Greek.

his applies to everyone and everything in Greece that
as not been internationalised. But outside the cities and
ackage hotels, the Greek Tourist Authority has imposed a
ort of uneasy conformity on restaurants and tavernas. In
onsequence, they all display a notice something like this:

'By this Order is necessary expose ourselves promi-
nently in Restaurant.
At often, persons of the Town shall visit Restaurant to
make inspexion all bodies in labor and to check tacks
on dishes.

All ofering dishes contain 15% tacks and 10% for them
in labor.
By this writen upwards we become Place of Licence
under Act of Public Dirtiness.'

My rich uncle rightly commented on one of these notices:
'Who would have expected to see "licence" properly spelt
in so remote a place?'

But there is another reason why Greek restauranteurs more
or less conform. It is simple and overwhelming. They have
no food.

What they do have is menus: vast and entrancing folders,
with every dish under the sun listed in Greek and a language fondly thought to be English. Some items are easily
deciphered:

Roast Lamp
Smacked Xam
Eal Catlets

Others become clear only as one masters the language:

Kalamaris
Kotopolo
Galatopourekko

But some are completely opaque:

Fried gazoil
Arico jumpers
Oppijops

Little of this is actually available. Ever since the Turks
departed, leaving a confused memory of intolerable oppres-
sion and a marvellous cuisine, amiable chaos has reigned.
Turkish coffee survived till the Cyprus Troubles, when it had
to be renamed Greek Coffee; then everyone thought: 'What
the hell?' (in Greek: 'What the Hades?') and drank a liquid
universally called *Nes*. Under the Hellenised menus lurks the
memory of real Greek food: bread and olives, sheep's cheese,
a pile of beans or whatever grows in a poor dry soil, and, with
luck, a chunk of lamb once a week.

PAUL GRIFFIN

Useful Phrases For Travellers

On the ferry to Ostend

Toegang: Football supporters through here.

Spui: For use of passengers in rough weather.

E.O. PARROTT

Germany

Aufsprungdurchtechnik: State-of-the-art flick-knife
Deutschland uber alles: German beer is best
Guten abend: Gone round the bend
Nicht wahr: Pyjamas

MARY HOLTBY

In Italy

La donna è mobile: The wife's got the car.

PETER VEALE

WFNW

Via Dolorosa:	Unmade-up road

E.O. PARROT

Literati:	Refuse collector

SUE SAXB'

In Spain

Auto da fe:	Fairy cycle
Por favor:	Do me a favour and be Mother

MARY HOLTB'

In France

Bidet:	June 4, 1944
Boulangerie:	Down with underwear
Je pense donc je suis:	I live on immoral earnings
Esprit de corps:	Embalming fluid
Café au lait:	Spanish coffee hits the spot
Route nationale:	Carrot
Plus ça change, plus c'est la même chose:	I'll have my change, if it's all the same to you
Poule de luxe:	Jacuzzi
Autres pays, autre moeurs:	If someone else is buying, I'll have another drink
Cache-sexe:	Prostitution
Nom de Guerre:	I am a photographer
Alimentation:	Islamic philosophy

BASIL RANSOME-DAVIES

Folie à deux:	Schizophrenia

LIONEL BURMAN

Défense de cracher:	Buffers
Biftec:	Third degree
Interpol:	A parrot's funeral

ARTHUR P. COX

Avoirdupois:	Do have some peas

E. O. PARROTT

Hors de Combat: The colonel's little bit on the side

Tour de force: Police outing
KATIE MALLETT

La vice anglaise: Black & Decker workmate
GEORGE SIMMERS

Film noir: You left the lens cap on
TIM BEECHAM

Ménage à trois: A very small zoo
BEN FRANCIS

Déjeuner sur l'herbe: Vegetarian meal
MONICA RIBON

Tant pis: Auntie's drunk
GERARD BENSON

Homme de lettres: Postman
PASCOE POLGLAZE

Belle laide

Belle laide:	Good in bed
Crie de coeur:	Bow-wow!
Amour propre:	Missionary position
Suivez la piste:	Follow that drunk
Belle esprit:	Scotch whisky

PETER VEALE

Après moi le deluge: I pulled the chain and look
       what happened!

MARY HOLTBY

Lament

Now that we're all European
'Ow I wish that I'd stuck at me French,
Me name might 'ave been up in neon
If I'd not been a bone-idle wench.

I'd 'ave wowed 'em in Paris twice-nightly
Wiv me witty an' wise Eurospeak,

In Athens 'ave shone just as brightly –
'avin' picked up a smatterin' of Greek.

The fellas 'd all 'ave chucked roses,
The girls 'd'ave all been green-eyed,
An' I'd 'ave been snapped in louche poses
For magazines sold Eurowide.

But the nights when I should 'ave been doin'
French 'omework, I'm sorry to say,
I was courtin' me downfall an' ruin
By makin' a good deal of 'ay.

So I'll never be toast of French caffs, nor
Yet of the smart set in Rome;
P'raps, like Wordsworth, I'll look at the daffs more
An' learn to speak proper at 'ome!

MARGARET ROGERS

Your Questions Answered

Q. *Where do European languages come from?*

To understand this, we have to go right back in history to the time of the dinosaurs and the pyramids. At that time, there were very few people indeed in Europe, apart from a few cavepersons, who spoke only in a grunting 'language' called **Trog**. It wasn't until Europe was invaded by the speaking peoples of India, Persia and Mongolia, that people actually began to talk amongst themselves in what we would nowadays recognise as words. The first word known to have been spoken in Europe is *Ecce*, and there are still some parts of Lancashire where this prehistoric greeting is used. Most of the early conversation concerned killing and dying, since everybody ate meat and most people died young.

Q. *Is this why dead languages are so called?*

Yes. There were two dead languages which sprang up: **Latin** and **Greek**. They are very similar, and together form the basis of nearly all the languages spoken today in Europe. However, this is not always obvious, because linguistic variation occurs. This is because different tribes needed secret codes in which to communicate their private ideas. The Germans, for instance were known as 'the salt of the earth' by the aristos in Rome (the first capital of Europe). The Latin for 'salt of the earth' is *terra saxa*, and the wilder common people came to be known as Saxons as a result. The Saxons invaded Britain (which is why we sound German when we have 'flu). Some German words still survive, as in the Scots phrase 'och aye.' The German for 'high' is '*hoch*', so the phrase is really 'hi hi', or in Glasgow, 'aye aye.'

Hoch aye

There are a few tribes on Europe's fringe who continue to speak in languages derived from codes so secret that, after a while, no-one could remember what they meant, tribal elders having forgotten to pass on the meanings. One of these is **Breton**, which is spoken in Brittany. Now if you say the word 'Breton' very quickly, you should notice that it *does* sound very like 'Britain'. This is why, on a clear day, Bretons can understand Welsh language speakers (Wales used to be called Small Britain before Great Britain existed). There is also **Cornish**, which is unfortunately a dead language now, although you still buy their famous clotted cream at Poldark Tregarras, their ancient capital.

Q. *Are there any other fringe languages?*
Yes. The most famous is **Basque**. This unusual language has given the rest of Europe many words, including *basket, biscuit, busker, tabasco,* and *basically*. Some think it is even related to Cornish (think of *The Hound of the Baskervilles*). **Lapp** is another very mysterious language, and is thought to derive from the need to speak very slowly and carefully because in Lapland, it is always snowing, and usually dark. **Gaelic** speakers were driven out of Gaul into the west of Ireland and the North of Scotland by those Latin aristos.

Two other strange languages are **Mafia**, which nobody talks about talking, but is thought to be spoken in Sicily, and **Geordie**, which is spoken on the banks of the Tyne by moving the *geor* (jaw) in a peculiar way.

Q. Will there ever be a single language spoken throughout Europe?
Yes, indeed. There are already plans for a Common European Linguistic Tongue (or **CELT**) to be in place shortly after the turn of the century. Ifa ich geçälle amt to spooken uno bitte du yon tjŒngk, ich thönck yu vilt llykelly undistini mio verbos widŒt mochâ dificilité. Actually, this is a simulation, but it is very like the sort of thing they are planning. Essentially Europranto (as it will colloquially be known) is an attempt to get back to the basic language spoken before all these secret codes confused everything.

Q. What language do they speak in Belgium?
Congo.

BILL GREENWELL

EUROCUSTOMS

One of the pleasures of European travel is the festivals. How the tourist's spirits lift on entering a European town to find the shops already closed in preparation for the fiesta! Here are some festivals uncovered by our correspondents.

The Festival Of The Farmers, Northern France

Nowhere in Europe is the contrast between city and country more marked than in France, and the Festival of the Farmers, which can take place at any time of year, is the countryman's traditional way of reminding urban folk of the agricultural heritage upon which they all depend.

The Festival takes many forms, but the element common to them all is the symbolic bestowal of agricultural produce upon the city-dwellers by the farming community. They may, for instance, distribute a thousand tons of turnips outside the Ministry of Agriculture as a token of thanks for the consideration they have received in the past and anticipate in the future. At another time the citizens at large may receive the gifts, as for instance when large quantities of mature cabbage are spread liberally throughout one of the fashionable shopping streets. Sometimes motorists are the beneficiaries, as when sheep carcasses are heaped on the roads approaching the city.

The Festival is not confined to Paris, however, or even to France. Tourists arriving at the Channel ports may find a welcoming cordon of tractors denoting that the Festival is in progress there. The Farmers in their picturesque blousons and berets, may be good-humouredly overturning egg-trucks in their eagerness to ensure that tourists rushing for the autoroutes linger awhile in the country regions. A particularly imaginative climax to one Festival 'happening' was the presentation of a live cow to the EEC Commissioners on the top floor of their headquarters building in Brussels.

All this, of course, is recognisable as a basic fertility rite, and is doubtless of considerable antiquity. Some authorities believe that after the French Revolution, when the Church was separated from the State, the farmers, deprived of the opportunity of paying tithes, assuaged their guilt by making the people the recipients of their bounty. In fact, the Festival may be much older even than this; the incident of the Brussels cow, elevated as it was both physically and hierarchically, suggests that the Festival may have its roots in a form of Hinduism imported by the Indo-European migrants in the 15th century BC.

Be that as it may – and it must be admitted that these theories are somewhat speculative – it need not cramp the enjoyment of the Festivities by the tourist with an eye for local colour. The farmers will usually pose for your camera, and may even wave their farm implements at you. If so, don't be afraid to greet them in their own language, praising their countryside with a cry of *'Paysan!'* (literally, 'Healthy Country!') or perhaps *'Ventre Bleu!'* ('May the Breeze Blow!'). You will be assured of a warm response.

The Festival Of Le Grand Départ, France

Many visitors to France about the end of July are puzzled to find a step-change in the pace of activity around them. They have been enjoying the extraordinary peace of the French countryside, the amazingly uncluttered roads, the villages with no sign of life; when suddenly, as at a pre-arranged signal, the roads are full of perspiring families in overloaded cars of all types and sizes, hurrying dangerously in all directions. What can have happened? A nuclear accident, perhaps? An extra-terrestrial invasion?

No. It is merely the festival of Le Grand Départ, which takes place annually on the first Saturday in August. It looks like a pre-arranged signal because it *is* a pre-arranged signal. On this day, by ancient and hallowed tradition, it is necessary for all French people to be somewhere else. Nor is this simply a desire to be near to the sea brought on by the warm weather, for visitors to the seaside are quite likely to be greeted by notices on hotels and restaurants advising them of the 'Fermeture Annuelle'; the proprietors have departed for their own somewhere else. City dwellers depart for the coast, coastal dwellers depart for the countryside, and country-dwellers depart for the towns.

The festival clearly ministers to some deep primitive instinct, perhaps harking back to the time of the Visigoths, or some other nomadic occupants of the country that is now France. However that may be, this is one festival which is not recommended for tourists. The French like to keep this one for themselves, and to venture out with GB plates showing appears to invite volleys of *'le klaxon'*, though to be fair it is not always easy to tell at whom these warnings are directed. All the same, it is a good weekend to spend with a couple of dozen Simenons.

The festival only lasts for the weekend, after which the movement is absorbed into the Campings and Plein-Airs until the corresponding weekend four weeks later, when the whole process is repeated, or rather reversed. The nomadic urge has then been sublimated for a further year.

The Festival Of The Lagelouts, Costa Brava, Spain

Spain has long played host to a variety of ethnic cultures. The Romany and Moorish civilizations both took root here many centuries ago and flourished in the hospitable Spanish sunshine. Of more recent origin, though equally obscure, is the annual Festival of the Lagelouts, which takes place each year in August along the Costa Brava.

The Lagelouts descend on the coast apparently guided only by oral tradition, much in the way that Gypsies congregate at horse-fairs. Nobody knows their place of origin, and the Lagelouts themselves don't seem to know where they have come from, how soon they are going back or, for that matter, where they are. An old local superstition even has it that they descend from the sky. Linguistic studies have detected a predominantly Northern European influence in their speech, and it has been suggested that their language is a relation of English, albeit a poor one. As with Bretons and Cornish people, there is a persistent tradition that the Lagelouts and the English can make themselves mutually understood, though when one listens closely to the Lagelouts, this is difficult to believe.

The Festival itself has no organised sequence of events, being essentially orgiastic in character. In this it may owe something to the Dionysan and Bacchic traditions of the ancient world, though the Lagelouts themselves know nothing of this, at least at the conscious level. One Lagelout I questioned did say he thought it was 'All fickin' Greek' to him, but it would be unwise to infer too much from this remark. A more likely origin might be found in the Orcadian mid-winter celebration of 'Up-helly', the Lagelout's midsummer counterpart having become by a simple process of euphony, 'Out-belly'.

Nevertheless, it is clear that Lagelout culture exhibits many of the most enduring features of primitive cultures found throughout the world. Sun-worship is an important element, even to the extent of merging into self-mutilation, as though the Lagelout is engaged in self-preparation as a burnt offering. An element of ritual cleansing is also present, as evidenced by the drinking of large quantities of liquid matter, which, since it is promptly regurgitated, clearly has a function more purgative than nutritive. One further aspect of Lagelout behaviour over which anthropologists are still puzzling is their unique custom of competitive copulation.

Lagelouts keep a tally of their 'score' during the festival, though investigators suggest that many of these 'scores' are unreliable, not to say plain impossible.

Unreliable Scores

However, it is not as a dry academic study but as a colourful piece of pageantry that the tourist can best appreciate the Lagelouts. In their exotic costumes – vests blazoned with strange messages, tri-coloured loin-pieces with their characteristic ethnic design, hair either rampant or cropped out of existence – they are unmistakable. If you follow them, at a safe distance, you may be privileged to hear their tribal chants: 'We ate not in um forest', for instance, harking back to who knows what primeval deprivations; or that fierce yet haunting song marking the rite of passage to manhood, 'You'll never wear cologne.'

There are those who would seek to 'civilise' the Lagelouts, to bring them into the modern world. To me, though, they represent an echo of less complex times, before the world was embroiled in such fiendish complexities as computers, space probes, and joined-up writing.

The Festival Of The Coro Dell'Alba, Rome

When visiting foreign countries, particularly when we are on holiday and in a relaxed mood, it is tempting to start the day a little later than usual. Visitors to Rome should try to resist this urge, at least on one or two occasions, for they run the risk of missing one of Rome's most spectacular sights and sounds, the *Coro dell'Alba*, or dawn chorus.

The Italians are an impetuous and life-loving people, and the return of daylight after the hours of darkness awakes in them an echo of the old festivals of Primavera, the celebration which used to accompany the return of Spring. The *Coro dell'Alba*, however, is a thoroughly modern affair. All over Rome the citizens, full of joy, jump into their cars or straddle their scooters and set out for the city centre. Gradually the roads and streets fill up until the entire city seems to be a mass of gaily-coloured vehicles. When the point is reached at which no further progress is possible and all the vehicles are stationary, the many-timbred horns, or 'trombe', begin to be heard, rising to a massive crescendo. The resulting sound, ascending above the city's ancient monuments, swirling and echoing round the Colosseum and the great dome of St Peter's, is something no tourist can ever forget.

The Festival Of The Air Traffic Controllers

This is one of the truly international festivals of Europe, transcending all national boundaries, for the Air Traffic Controllers are an international brotherhood. The festival usually takes place in the summer months, in late July or August, though it can sometimes happen quite spontaneously at other times such as April or late December.

The Air Traffic Controllers are a secretive cult, and their arcane rituals are jealously guarded from the eyes of people outside the order. They are, however, a charitable foundation whose purposes are to shield the traveller from harm in the tradition of St Christopher. It is necessary for them, therefore, to reimpose the purity of their discipline from time to time, and this is the reason for the festivals. At these times the Air Traffic Controllers go back to the fundamentals of their beliefs, reasserting the primacy of the Book in everything they do. For the duration of the Festival all their words and deeds are dictated by absolute adherence to the literal text which holds the key to their faith, and which no outsider has seen. At the end of the festival the Air Traffic Controllers emerge renewed and rewarded.

Naturally, the lay traveller may be occasionally inconvenienced by the festivals, but he may rest assured in the knowledge that the renewal of faith is in the direct interest of his travelling safety. Indeed, it can be claimed that safety is outstandingly high at festival times, for not only is the Air Traffic Controllers' vigilance at its height, but many would-be travellers have their safety secured by ensuring that the part of their journey which involves actual movement through the air is avoided altogether.

The Ceremony Of The Blessing Of The Imports, Poitiers, France

France, although lacking the ceremonial splendours associated with a Royal family, has, nevertheless, a number of fascinating and rewarding traditions in its more ancient cities. One of the most interesting is that which takes place every day in the Customs Centre at Poitiers in Western France: the Ceremony of the Blessing of the Imports.

The goods to be blessed are brought to Poitiers – which is some distance inland – by road, but are not technically on French soil until they have been inspected, blessed and cleared. Each item, which may be a Japanese video-recorder or a Taiwanese microwave oven, for instance, is brought before one of the *douaniers*, who scrutinises the box with great care and reads details from the the accompanying papers aloud to the assistant *douanier*. Then, flanked by two assistant *douaniers*, he turns smartly and walks with measured tread to the other end of the Customs shed, a distance of some two hundred metres. He halts before the chief *douanier*, salutes, and says, 'Video 5657349 inspected and approved. Permission to release requested.' The chief *douanier* stands, draws his sword and returns the Douanier's salute; and bows his head in symbolic granting of the request. The *douanier*, still flanked by his two assistants, then processes back to the other end of the shed and pronounces the Video-recorder free to enter the Republic of France. The whole ceremony, which takes little more than ten minutes, is then repeated for the next package.

The ceremony has its origins in a more turbulent past, when it was necessary to protect the French people from the importation of undesirable items such as New Zealand butter or hydrogen bombs. Nowadays it remains as an interesting survival of days gone by. It is generously sponsored by French manufacturing companies to ensure that the gentler ways of the past are not entirely forgotten.

The Berlin Wall Game

The Berlin Wall Game is quite unlike the famous Eton Wall Game in that it involves the actual destruction of the wall. This is necessarily a slow process, however, and the tourist anxious to catch a glimpse of this picturesque custom can be assured that it is likely to continue for many years yet.

It can be seen at any time in most stretches of the wall, but is particularly active at the weekends, when large numbers of Berliners gather with picks and other small implements to chip away pieces of the wall. These are then taken away to their homes, which in every case are furnished with equipment for embedding the fragments in clear plastic, and printing presses for printing Certificates of Authenticity. The embedded fragments are then sold internationally, and it seems entirely possible that the wall will prove to be large enough to provide such a memento for every desk and mantelpiece in the world. In this respect the wall may eventually take on a significance similar to that of the True Cross, fragments of which were such a staple of international commerce in the middle ages.

Although the Wall Game can be regarded as a competitive sport, there is no formal declaration of a winner. Among the adherents of the game, however, any player who has accumulated a million marks from wall-related activities is accorded considerable respect. For this reason the Wall Game also has a deep economic and political significance; for the East Berliner travelling West, it is his first glimpse of the miracle of how the market economy works for the universal benefit of mankind.

NOEL PETTY

Your Questions Answered

Q. Where does Santa Claus live?
As you can probably see from his name, Santa Claus
was originally Spanish (think of Santa Cruz), but he
is a TRUE European. His reindeer are from Iceland, but
their names, Doner (Greek), Blitzen (German), Bambi
(Dutch) and Prancer (English) show just how Euro-
politan Santa is. In some countries, his name has been
corrupted over the years until it has become 'Saint
Nicholas' or 'Father Christmas'. These kinds of changes
come about because we all speak in slightly different
dialects, and they are just part of the rich tapestry that
comprises our continent. As for where Santa lives, it
is no secret that he lives at the North Pole, which is in
Denmark.

Q. Who is the patron saint of Europe?
St Alban, chosen by Brussels because he has his head
in his hands. In Britain, he is sometimes known as
St Hemel of Hempstead, although it is not known
why.

Q. What is the Orthodox church?
Basically, this is a very ordinary church, very plain,
with no steeples, flying buttresses, frescoes, vestries,
pantries, fonts or anything like that. In fact, it's just an
'orthodox' building. It could be a bus station, or even
a beach-hut. Orthodox churches do not worry about
prayers, hymns, holy water or doctrinal disputes. They
just get on with it, although there is one rule, which is
that priests must wear black and grow beards. You can
find an orthodox church in Greece (the **Greek Orthodox**), Belgium (the **Walloon Orthodox** and the **Fleming
Orthodox**) and also in Liverpool (the **Liverpooldox**).

Q. What are the national costumes of each country?
The Spanish wear a whisk at the waist known as a
Spanish Fly; the Germans wear a hat with a feather

in it, known as a **Deutsch Cap**; the Greeks wear a
tunic called a **Hella**, but only on feast days (the rest
of the time they are locked away upstairs – 'Hellas
– from the Attic'.) The Italians dress for emphasis in
Italics, beautiful togas which slope from left to right.
The British wear shirts and trousers called **Separates**.

Q. *What are the national dances?*
The Irish dance the **Jig**. The British dance the **Morris**.
The French dance the **Citroën** (in which oranges and
lemons are pressed). The Germans dance the very
graceful **Benz**. The Spanish and Portuguese dance the
High Sierra. The Italians dance the **Fiat Uno**. And the
Greeks dance the **Domestica**.

Q. *What are the most famous dishes?*
Contrary to public belief, the French do not subsist
entirely on but frogs and snails. Their national dish is
crapaud dans le trou, which I believe is very scrummy.
The Spaniards eat ***cordobes***, or bully beef. Danes eat

bacon in butter; Greeks eat *feta*, the hooves of local goats. Germans usually eat *brot*, a fish. In Italy, *pisa puddini* is very popular with locals and tourists alike. The Irish serve a wonderful dish of potatoes stewed in Guinness and scrag juice, known locally as *shebeen*.

Q. What are the national instruments?

In Greece, the principal instrument is a **bazooka**, which is played throughout the day, but never on Sunday. The Italians have many instruments – the **cello**, the **viola**, the **cornetto**, the **piano**, the **forte** and the **diminuendo**. Germans are famous for the **handel**, a barrel-organ, and for the **gato**, a Black Forest speciality. The Belgians play percussive instruments like the **hergé** and **tin-tin**. Dutch folk play the **windmill**, heard to great effect on their National Anthem, the 'Hollandaise'. The Spanish play the **olé**, a thin reedy pipe, and the French play the **cor anglais**.

Q. Will Europe ever have a king or queen?

Really, this is a family matter for our queen. You may not realise this, though there is a royal family in every country in Europe, though some of them got bored and handed in their crowns many years ago. In Holland, the royal family goes shopping on bicycles, and the King of Portugal wears a funny hat and tells ribald stories on street corners. The locals salute their royals, but nothing more. They are all related to each other, and to our Queen, who is related to herself in fifteen different ways. Her as-it-were unemployed cousins are known in Debrett's as 'cousins once removed' (like King Constantinopoulos of Greece). Probably King Charles III will be crowned monarch of the continent next century.

BILL GREENWELL

EUROCULTURE

The aspiring European should be well acquainted with his cultural and historical inheritance. This is a very wide field to cover and should be taken gradually. Here are some of the salient points to get you started.

The culture of the Ancient Greeks
   Unites all Europe, so it's said;
And yet how rare it is one speaks
   Of all those celebrated dead;
For Agamemnon, Paris, Helen,
Find little place in Tring or Welwyn.

If you discuss the goddess Hera,
   Compare her lightly with Astarte,
You'll not make conversation clearer
   In any pub or sherry party;
Legends are dead where life is hectic,
Material, and dialectic.

Better recall those other Greeks,
   Fathers of science and research:
So leave Demeter as she seeks
   Persephone by beech and birch
For Archimedes, bath towel round him,
Who ran the streets and cried: 'I've *found* him!'

It's true the gods were far more flighty;
   They loved their triangles of love:

Hephaistos once with Aphrodite
   Netted poor Ares from above;
But this has lost its power to stagger us:
For triangles, we need Pythagoras.

And as for nets, why, let us give
   Our thoughts to Eratosthenes
Whose justly celebrated Sieve
   Possesses virtue that can please;
For in a way that outlasts time
It shows which numerals are Prime.

Pierian Muses, sink your breath
   Into your fountain's deepest basement;
Galen will certify your death
   And Archimedes your displacement;
For now, when verse is in request,
Euclid's name will be addressed.

Farewell then, nymphs of trees and springs;
   Farewell to you, O Cytherean;
Let ancient scientists be kings —
   They too were born in the Aegean:
Theirs the uniting culture sent
To countries of our continent.

PAUL GRIFFIN

Lost Marbles

When Britain and Greece and the rest
Put full market links to the test
Will the Greeks count the cost
Of the marbles they lost
Or think they are jointly possessed?

KATIE MALLETT

Though the Venus de Milo is armless
She's nevertheless far from charmless.
   Even chiselled in stone
   Her erogenous zone
Is highly suggestive, if harmless.

STANLEY J. SHARPLESS

History Repeated

One day, in a field near Pompeii,
Edward lay with his girl in the hay.
When Vesuvius erupted
She cried out: 'Get up, Ted –
I don't want to get stuck this way!'

E.O. PARROTT

The Romance Of The Rose – An Insight

Some European countries consider that they possess indig-
enous cultures, and it seemed important at this stage to
understand them. I therefore wrote to an educated French
lady, asking if she would explain one of their great poems of
the Middle Ages. This was her reply:

You demand me that I describe the intrigue of the
grand French poem of middle age: 'The Romance of
the Rose'. It necessitates first that you comprehend
figures of metaphor. When the poet visits the Garden
of Funny Laughter it does not concern itself nor with
poet nor with garden. It is the life that is figure.
   After deities disporting, one bud of rose has spotted

itself to our man, in a basin where jets of water propel themselves. He sees not the bud but as in a mirror. The rose is figure of dame. Our poet wishes to arrive at her, but he is interfered with by personages not truly personages: Ashamedness, Boss, Incorrect Seeming, Thinkful, and Jealousness.

Cupidon shoots at him flitches and depends our man to him. His advice how to penetrate? One must find servile female and corrupt her with winepot.

But jealousness becomes constructor and undertakes battlements in surround of the desired. Alas! no penetration!

Not all there, is what to comprehend of these figures, of the dames, of the belief, of the society; but that which rests gives much severity.

PAUL GRIFFIN

A Very Early Tourist

At King Arthur's court, bold Sir Lancelot
And Queen Guinevere used to dance a lot,
   They both got so zealous
   That Arthur grew jealous,
So he sent Lancelot off to France a lot

STANLEY. J. SHARPLESS

When Giotto
Got blotto
His sense of perspective
Became defective.

RON RUBIN

I learned in an art class
That G.A. Beltraffio
Copied his master,
Adhered to his style.

His master, da Vinci,
Said: 'That's enough flattery –
Imitate somebody
Else for a while.'

BRUCE E. NEWLING

'That's enough flattery . . .'

Christopher Columbus
Wasn't much good at rumbas,
But as for his samba –
Caramba!

RON RUBIN

Airily-fairily
Madame de Maintenon
Made the remark, 'After me comes the flood'.
Did she foresee, maybe,
Ultraclairvoyantly
Guillotines dripping with upper-class blood?

BASIL RANSOME-DAVIES

M. Guillotin made his Rex ex.
He divided, and ruled, either sex.
    His capital cutter
    Would slice, as through butter,
Pierres from their Robes, and their nex.

BILL GREENWELL

As Asia is the source of copra,
A coconut derivative,
So Italy's the home of opera:
It really hits them where they live.
An ultra-extroverted nation,
Their attitude is 'play it loud',
And calm, reflective contemplation
Is not for them. They like a crowd.
While *Rigoletto* or *Aida*
May blow their minds in Rome and Florence,
I'd rather sit and quietly read a
Mucky book by D. H. Lawrence.

BASIL RANSOME-DAVIES

Clattery, battery,
Ludwig van Beethoven
Banged on the keyboard, re-
Gardless of clef;

Some thought his music was
Superterrestrial,
Others said crossly: 'The
Man must be deaf.'

MARY HOLTBY

Although Louis Pasteur
Was an obsessive voyeur,
He'd much rather watch the fermentation of cheese
Than strip-tease.

RON RUBIN

Said Gaugin, inflamed by *vin sec*:
'Paris gives me a pain in the neck.
  I'm off to Tahiti
  Where the girls are more meaty;
I've nothing Toulouse but Lautrec.'

STANLEY J. SHARPLESS

You cannot hope to warp or twist
The vision of a Dadaist,
Who turns into subversive jokes
What makes good sense to normal blokes.
Why bother to unhinge his brain?
The man's already quite insane.

BASIL RANSOME-DAVIES

'I can't make out what that is,'
Complained Matisse;
'Is thasso?'
Replied Picasso.

GERARD BENSON

The Stalinisation of Albania
Was a sort of a mania
Of Enver Hoxha.
He was a terrible old coxha.

PAUL GRIFFIN

O, Mann!

Niminy-piminy,
Gustav von Aschenbach
Sighs for a stripling
As seaward he slips;

Torn by this touch of the
Extracurricular,
Takes to cosmetics and
Hands in his chips.

MARY HOLTBY

Observe this photograph of Munich:
The *Führer* in a well-cut tunic
And Chamberlain demure beneath
His spectacles, moustache and teeth.
A European love affair!
Yet all too soon the happy pair
(So fickle is the human heart)
Discovered they were Poles apart.

BASIL RANSOME-DAVIES

higgledy-piggledy
Cinéma vérité
Took the approach of a fly on the wall
With the result that its
Cinematography
Captured the essence of nothing at all

BASIL RANSOME-DAVIES

Hoitily-toitily
Victor Emmanuel
Told Mussolini, 'I'm ending our fling.'
As a result of his
Impetuosity
Italy now has no Duce or King.

BASIL RANSOME-DAVIES

From the land of the sild and the brisling
Came a venomous traitor called Quisling.
Does he know that his name
Is a symbol of shame,
In the hell where he's currently sizzling?

BASIL RANSOME-DAVIES

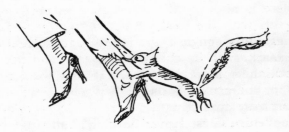

Your Questions Answered

Q. *Is there a connection between the Common Market and the Eurovision Song Contest?*

Yes. A long and proud one. An early winner of the Song Contest was the Copenhagen songstress, Dana, for instance. The Spanish entry by Massiel won the competition with a song written entirely in French ('*La la la, la la la*'). The French singer, Lulu, once won the competition with a wonderful ditty about the likely consequences of excessive consumer expenditure upon the exchange markets, a number called 'Boom Bang-a-Bang' which had a profound effect upon EEC thinking. There is something surprising, perhaps this question hints, at the fact that Morocco, Israel, Turkey and Yugoslavia, amongst others, are involved. Well, all one can say is that, if they are not 'in Europe', they SHOULD be, and they are bound to join the Common Market one day soon. So the Eurovision Song Contest is always looked upon as a very forward-looking, even prophetic institution. That is why one perennial loser is a spoof country called 'The Ostrich' '*L'Autriche*') – it's Europe's way of telling the world that we should not stick our heads in the sand.

Q. *What is the cultural capital of Europe?*

Most emphatically, **Venice**. This is the haunting city where such classics as *Don't Look Now, Death In Venice, The Sea, The Sea* and *The Riddle of the Sands* were set. There is nothing like wandering its narrow cobbled streets with the local guides, the gondoliers, singing their merry songs. There is the beautiful Cathedral of St Mark, with its cheerful *campanile* and her pigeons flocking to meet you. There is that wonderful cloth shop, the Harris Bar, where tweed is woven before your very eyes. This is where the Doge ruled, where the Venice Glass hangs beneath the Bridge of Sighs, where the Venice de Milo was found, where blinds were invented, and where Ruskin sat eating the local delicacy – stag, or *venison* as we know it. A city that should be on *everyone's* itinerary!

BILL GREENWELL

. . . flock to meet you . . .

EUROCRATS

The administrative centres of the EEC, in Brussels and Strasbourg, have sometimes attracted unfavourable comment from uninformed sections of the British press. The good European will ignore this; one has only to look at the work of these bodies in detail to see that it is solely for our benefit.

A Contract For Fish Sticks

It is not true that life in the EEC is more complicated than it used to be. To prove the point, here is part of the new, simplified form of the contract required by those people who wish to purchase fish sticks. These contracts may be signed, witnessed and ratified in the presence of a member of the EEC legal department at most supermarket check-outs. What could be more straightforward than that?

MEMORANDUM of Agreement made this . . . . . day of . . . . . 19.. between . . . . . (hereinafter called the purchaser) of the first part and . . . . . . (hereinafter called the vendor) of the second part.

WHEREBY it is mutually agreed as follows respecting an item of comestibles required by the said purchaser and at present known as 6 FRY-UP FISH STICKS, hereinafter referred to as the goods.

1. The vendor shall during the legal term defined by the sell-by date provide the purchaser with the goods at a price not greater than . . . . . .

2. The vendor may offer the goods at a discount which may (or may not) vary between 15% and 3% of the recommended retail price at any moment up to and including a valid check-out, which shall be defined by the point mid-way between the entrance to the check-out channel and its exit. A check-out shall be deemed to be valid when a check-out person is in attendance at a till.

2a. A check-out person shall be identified by a plastic lapel badge which may (or may not) bear the name or identification of that person. The check-out person shall be considered to be in attendance at a till when seated and signed on by a supervisor. (See EEC form SM/003/5 for regulations governing relations between supervisors and check-out persons.)

2b. The purchaser hereby agrees not to enter into conversation with a check-out person.

3. The purchaser hereby warrants to the vendor that the said goods shall be referred to only as FISH STICKS and not as FISH FINGERS or by any other name regardless of the fact that such a name may contain the word FISH.

4. The vendor hereby agrees to consume the said goods on or before the sell-by date. The consumption of the goods shall only be deemed valid when completed by the named purchaser or by other persons referred to by name in clause 17c.

N.J. WARBURTON

Lingua Franca

'If only we spoke a common tongue', I sighed,
Brooding over the European map;
'We've got one already', the Brussels man replied,
'In daily use. We call it Eurocrap'.

STANLEY J. SHARPLESS

Food for Thought

When the animal's dead
And they've cut off his head
And the rest has gone off for its quartering,
You will see at your feet
A mass of 'Green Meat' –
For that's what they call it in Slaughtering.

We in Feeds are not fools:
We know all the rules
Which forbid using Green Meat for food,
So we send it away
To a firm near Marseilles
On whose business we never intrude.

I can't undertake
To say what they make;
If I asked them I doubt if they'd tell it;
They're all part, you see,
Of 'Hans Gartner A. G. –
Eurocake, Eurograin, Europellet!'

The meal we import
Is a very good sort
Sent from Gartners, just south of Treviso;
It's a quality feed
Of a kind guaranteed
By a paper that swears it to be so.

In your magazine, please
Don't speak of disease;
Think of each Euro-state as a partner;
This affair's made our boss
So terribly cross.
You'd like him. His name is Hans Gartner.

PAUL GRIFFIN

Harmonisation of Breathing

In spite of strenuous government denials, there is a very strong rumour in Brussels that, following on from the Euro-standards applied to air pollution, the lung intake of every adult individual is to be graded, on a scale from one to ten. (Children under the age of 18 will be exempt from the grading, which it is thought will eventually result in a new air tax). A fully grown 6 foot, 16 stone weightlifter is thought to have a lung capacity of 9.62 litres, to put him at the top of the scale at ten, whereas a small-boned woman would have a capacity of only 3.1 litres at the rating of one.

First to receive the grading (by means of an external valve device) will be the members of the Europarliament, followed closely by each country's representatives in the home parliaments.

Members of the British Parliament are said to be worried about the effect of hot air on the dials, and have demanded a recount.

Meanwhile, electronic measuring device manufacturers are secretly getting ready for the new regulation, under cover of making pumps for central heating systems.

The Green Party have expressed an interest, stating that tax rebates should be available for those compelled to breathe polluted air.

KATIE MALLETT

Though Euro-MPs want it *their* ways,
They seldom agree which are fair ways,
    But their comings and goings
    In various Boeings
Are a wonderful boon for the airways.

PAUL GRIFFIN

From the Office of the European Commissioner for Culture.

AN ORDER OF SERVICE FOR A MEETING TO PLAN AN EXCHANGE VISIT
BETWEEN THE CHOIRS OF ANY TWO TWINNED TOWNS IN EUROPE

When any such visit is to be planned, the committee of
the host choir shall gather around the dining table of The
Chair, who shall be of either gender and shall for many years
have maintained a relationship of bantering distrust with The
Conductor.

The Chair shall ask whether anyone has heard from
Donald, who is supposed to have collected brochures
extolling the beauty of the locality from the Council Offices
and there shall be negative, humorously irritated murmurings
from those present.

Then shall The Chair say:
DEARLY beloved, forasmuch as it is two years since we visited
n or m, it has come to pass that the choir of n or m is to pay
us a return visit.

The People shall respond,
Oh God, not again!
OR:
Doesn't time fly, is it really two years?
OR:
Heavens, I've been meaning to write and thank Françoise
and now she'll be here before I get round to it.
OR:
Just when I've got the builders in.

The Chair, smiling tolerantly, shall continue,
Whereas two years ago we sang Elijah with the choir of n or
m in the cathedral of n or m, now it shall come to pass that
they will join with us in doing Messiah in the great squash
court at the sports centre.

And The People shall respond,
I enjoyed Messiah – the first hundred and fifty times.

OR:
The squash court brings on my hay fever.
OR:
Can they sing English well enough?
OR:
Is Ian conducting, or their man?

And the Chair shall say,
Their man, it is his turn.

And with one voice the people shall say,
It'll go on all night.

And The Chair shall say,
Verily we are not here to talk about music, for unless we
get down to planning a programme there will be a vain and
sanguinous shambles. There remaineth a scant five weeks
before the Itinerary must be typed and photocopied and sent
to n or m, and ere that time shall have elapsed we must book
the coaches and any other transport which may be deemed
meet, fix the reception with the Mayor . . .

The people shall cry,
Those awful long speeches!

The Chair shall implacably continue,
. . . and decide who shall be responsible for the food.

And The Conductor shall intervene thus,
May I point out through The Chair that I shall expect two full
rehearsals each week unto the time of the visitation so that
we may most certainly and confidently show them that we
are a better choir than they are.

And Some One shall say,
We can sing Messiah in our sleep.

And The Conductor shall riposte,
Yea, verily, and doth it sound like it!

Amidst laughter The Chair shall remark,
Witty as ever Ian. But we must renounce light and foolish
pleasures. What dost Thou, Treasurer, have to say?

The Treasurer, in a voice rich with years of cigars and cautionary speeches, shall declare,
These international high jinks always go over budget. If this one runs true to form the sinking fund will sink out of sight.

And The Librarian shall muse,
I suppose we do have to invite them.

And The Chair shall say,
The invitation was given formally at the end of the post-concert dinner at n or m two years ago. Verily, if we renege, World War Three will erupt. Forasmuch as they will arrive on the Friday Night in two batches according to when they can get off work, we shall meet them, take them to our several homes and give them a good meal.

And the Deputy-Treasurer shall say,
They fed and watered us well last time.

And The Chair shall say,
Exactly my point, brethren. It behoveth us not to let the side down.

And the Publicity Person shall say,
Fridays is my Origami class.

And the Chair shall say,
Dost thou believe in International Goodwill? Then must Thou renounce all private convenience. Saturday morning there shall be a rehearsal of all the choruses . . .

And the Treasurer shall interpose,
With or without orchestra?

And the Conductor shall respond,
Can we afford it with?

And The Treasurer shall state,
No.

The Chair shall continue,
. . . Saturday afternoon shall be free with the proviso that if the morning goes badly we shall rehearse again. The Concert

is in the evening. That looks after Saturday. Sunday night is the Mayoral Reception. Which leaves just that day to fill up.

The Federation Person shall say,
They took us sailing on Lake n or m.

And The Secretary shall say,
I enjoyed that. The buffet was smashing.

And The Publicity Person shall say,
What about the canal?

And The Treasurer shall say,
We can't crowd them on to a public boat and a special hire will cost a bomb.

And the Federation Person shall say,
We have to push the boat out sometimes. As it were.

And The Chair shall ask,
Would the Council give us a grant, do you think? Seeing it's a twinning project.

The People shall laugh hollowly.

The Librarian shall say,
It will probably rain. It usually does.

And The Chair shall say,
It rained when we were on Lake n or m, remember. I was quite pleased. I didn't feel so bad about our weather.

Then shall The Chair smile brightly, say that much useful progress has been made and declare the meeting closed.

TOM AITKEN

Eurobaffled

The E.R.M. fills all my dreams,
The ECU haunts my nights.
I spend my hours of fitful sleep
In frantic fiscal flights.
From deutschmarks to the gallic franc,
And lira to the schilling,
I try to fathom out what's what
(Mind weak, though spirit willing).

But really, all I want to know,
When all is said and done,
Is what my pound coin will be worth
When the Eurograb's begun.

KATIE MALLETT

Must I alone ask it:
Why in a basket?
What have matters monetary
To do with punnetry?

MARY HOLTBY

Your Questions Answered

Q. Why is The Common Market so called?
Because it replaced an organisation called The Common Wealth. There is a great deal of confusion about this. Joining the Market did not mean that Britain lost its Wealth, merely that it had to share it with others. Of course, the others have to share what was formerly *their* Wealth with us (which, if you think of Germany, is not too bad).

Q. What is The Treaty of Rome all about?
Probably you are thinking about The Treaty of **Frome** (an easy mistake to make). Frome is a Somerset village in which the locals struck a bargain whereby they could make a new cheese, in honour of the Common Market, which was a mixture of French Brie and Danish Blue. (The cheese is soft and sticky, like Brie, but with tangy blue bits in it.) The locals got permission, but their original choice of name, **'Fromage'**, had to be turned down when it was discovered that there was already a little-known French cheese of the same name. It is now called Lymeswold, after a local farmer, and very nice it is, too.

Q. What does the European Parliament do?
This august institution lies at the Common Market's heart, and takes care of all the political matters. For instance, it has to decide where each country's borders lie, how many political parties there are, and who should sit with whom when they're discussing important issues (like Borders). This is not easy. For instance, the word 'Liberal' means something very different in each country. The European Parliament has to sort out the Right-Wing liberals from the Left-Wing Liberals, and that takes patience. The Parliament also has to pass Laws, for instance that only Britain could call its Ice Cream 'Ice Cream' where everyone else had to call it 'Vegetable Fat'. Perhaps this example shows

you just how important the European Parliament is. It also does a lot of food tasting, which is vital for our health.

Q. *What is an EEC Commissioner?*

Commissioners are appointed to see if any countries are committing crimes which break European Laws. Europe has its very own court, the European Court of Human Rights, and the commissioners make sure that no country is committing a Wrong. After all, you can't have a proper European country filling its prisons with innocent victims, as in South America. So when, for instance, Spain applied to join the Common Market, the commissioners went straight round and said 'That's enough of this Inquisition business', and they had to stop it there and then.

Incidentally, commissioners are known by the country from which they come. Ours is called Sir Lion Britain, and is the son of the very famous Vera Britain.

Q. *What is the Common Fisheries Policy?*

There are several rules which govern fishing in Europe. For instance, Luxembourg is entirely forbidden to send out fishing-boats, because it has no border with the sea. There is a minimum mesh size, so that sprats, tiddlers, sticklebacks, dolphins and other small fish are not hunted to extinction (this is where the phrase 'net catch' comes from; gross catches are entirely against the rules). There was some resistance to this Policy at first, especially in those states where they had been using sprats to catch mackerel, but the sprat is now thought to be safe. The prawn cocktail is the only small fish that trawlers are allowed to hunt, since it is so popular, and a quick look inside every European restaurant will confirm that there are plenty to go round.

Entirely Forbidden

Q. What is 'The Snake'?

The Snake (or, to give it its full name, the European Monetary Snake) is the way money is kept in order inside the Common Market. In Brussels a large wicker contraption (the so-called Basket of Currencies) is hung from the ceiling of the central counting-room. In it there are special compartments, each of which is filled daily with one mark, one franc, one peseta, one 10p and so on. At eleven o'clock, and on the hour until teatime, news is flashed to Brussels about how much money is being spent in every European country. If (for instance) Germany is spending more than everyone else, then a small weight is added to the German compartment, and a note is made of the fact. Then, and this is the clever bit, a small weight is added to all the other compartments, so that all the currencies are equal, news of which is sent to all the exchanges, *cambios* and *wechsels*.

It is called 'The Snake' because the person who puts in the weight is known as an 'adder' (in France the official is known as *le chevalier*, a play on *ajouter* (to add) and *jouter* (to joust) – just one more example of

how rich and diverse our senses of humour are in the
European Community.)

Q. *Will Europe have its own currency one day?*
After no end of argument between the member states,
this question has now definitely been decided. Every
single country will have an **ECU** (European Cash
United) – *ecu* actually *means* money in France, so
this is indeed a happy coincidence. In Britain, the
ECU will be known as a '**pound**', in Germany a '**mark**',
in France a '**franc**', in Italy '**lire**', in Spain a '**peseta**', in
Greece a '**drachma**' and in Ireland a '**doubloon**'. The
others are still deciding, although Belgium is believed
to have opted for the '**poirot**'.

Q. *Will we all have to measure things differently in Europe?*
Of course. But there is no need to be afraid, because
other countries will have just as much difficulty adopting
some of our measurements (it is a rule that we have
to share things out fairly). Although we will have to
use 'avoirdupois' to weigh our vegetables, this will
also tax the Greeks who naturally wished to use Troy
weights. Besides, some of the changes are not nearly as
mysterious as they seem – **hectares** is just an anagram
of **the acres**. It would be nice if we could do this with
all measurements, but **inches** is an anagram of **chiens**,
and this might well lead to some confusion!

Q. *Will we get rabies when we join the Single Market?*
Rabies is carried by the continental bunny, the **rabit**,
and it has sometimes been known to spread through
contaminated lettuce. In Europe, however, the main
party is called The Greens, and they hope to have it
under control soon.

Q. *What is the French agricultural policy of 'remembrement'?*
I forget.

BILL GREENWELL

EUROCHARGE

All over Britain 1992 fever is beginning to stir, as all sections of society prepare.

The book world has not been slow to rise to the challenge of Europe. It has, however, had some hard thinking to do about its usual lines of best-sellers. How can these be made more European? How, in particular, can the Royal Family be made to fit the bill?

Here are some extracts from a few of the forthcoming Euro-friendly titles soon to be found in our bookshops:

Diary of a European Country Lady

June 4th ... Tea and crumpets after a gruelling day under the lights filming our Christmas message. We can't remember it taking so long before. Probably because we had to repeat the whole thing in a succession of the most throat-wrenching languages. Really, we felt as if we were trying to spit our tonsils out half the time. We hope the translation people have done their job properly. We have no idea what we were saying most of the time but some of it *sounded* rather rude.

June 11th ... A sweet little toady from Euro-channel came round with what he called the 'rushes'. It all sounded awfully urgent. P went off in a huff and wouldn't watch. He says he doesn't hold with talking to wops, frogs and the like. It's all right for him, though. He doesn't have to 'front the show' and can get by with standing around with his hands behind his back and looking faintly bored.

We don't mind being monarch of a complete country but to be a monarch of one *part* of a community is really spreading royalty rather too thinly in our opinion. After all, our country is very good at royalty. And royalty, we feel, is something we can offer to the rest of Europe. Must make a note of that for next year's broadcast. (We did suggest to the toady that it might be 'cut in' this year but he would say nothing but 'No way'. Apparently they'd have to trim something off the Christmas message of the EEC Commissioners and it would take till Easter to work out what.)

June 15th ... We have had a chat with the family and they've come up with some jolly good suggestions which might help to make Europe a kingdom rather than a mere community. D says community does sound so *common*. The Common Market, full of commoners. She can't really believe that that is what our subjects *really* want. (Good, coming from her, we thought.) The PR suggested that we might dabble in a little export business. Some countries in Europe have never had a proper monarch of their very own, she said. Or, as we pointed out to her, they have somehow managed to lose them. Anyway, we have plenty of spares and perhaps we ought to be prepared to loan some out on a long-term basis. E is young but could probably rule a smallish country quite nicely and wouldn't be missed terribly ...

The Royal Adventures of Dibby the Dago

Hallo. It's terrifically easy to write a book for kiddies and to prove it I've whizzed a few off for you. They're all about the Euro-thing and they're bags of jolly fun too. If you know a kiddie why not get hold of it and read it one of these wonderfully original yarns, OK? As well as Dibby the Dago, there's Fudgie the Frog and Kobbo the Kraut. There might be a few more too when they let me know what the other Euro-places are. Well, that's enough from me, so on with the exciting story of Dibby and how he comes to fancy a sweet little thing called . . . Chuddy, I think it was. Or Cruddy. Anyway, here goes –

'One day, as Dibby was bobbing along . . .'

(This is probably enough to give a flavour. Ed.)

A Vision of Europe

During one's travels in Europe, one has been appalled at the absolute bloody awful state of buildings in some European countries. (This includes ours, one has to say.) Bits of stone lying about all over the place in Athens, ugly great iron contraptions sticking up in the middle of Paris. That kind of thing. Absolute bloody disgrace. You might think that that's what you want but, one can assure you, you don't. Not really.

This is why one is starting a 'Prince's Vision of Europe' Fund and top of the list is that ghastly monstrosity in Pisa. Not only does the thing look like a stack of fastfood pizzas (hence the name, very probably) but it's also not even up straight. Bloody shoddy workmanship, no two ways about it, and it ought to be put to rights . . .

N. J. WARBURTON

1992 On the Newsstands

Editorials from a selection of magazines and newspapers

Women's Weekly

1992 is just around the corner. But that doesn't mean we'll all have to put garlic into our homely cottage pies, and olive oil on everything. Europe is more than just strange foreign food and people with dark eyes who wave their arms about when they talk. In the next few weeks we're going to look at what 1992 means to *Women's Weekly* readers, with serious articles on European knitting – the latest yarns: Crumpets and crêpes – tasty tea-time treats from Cremona to Cleethorpes: and short stories set where the language is Romance. All you need to know about Europe from your favourite weekly.

Cosmopolitan
1992 – and the barriers are down to Europe's hottest men. With easier travel you can have a lover in every EEC state and still run your London-based company. Worried about your stamina (and who wouldn't be with all Europe asking for it!)? Follow Cosmo's 5-day Euro-diet, and you'll be ready for anyone – anywhere.

Amateur Gardening
1992 won't spell the end of clematis wilt, carrot fly, or clubroot, but will give us a chance to swap 'tips and wrinkles' with gardeners across the Channel. When the fences come down you see more of folk, and can pick up some handy ideas. In next week's issue the French show us they know their onions, and our eesi-pull-out supplement is on Dutch ways with cabbage. Will calabrese crop in Catalonia? Does deutzia do well in Dusseldorf? Can buddleia blossom in Bari? Look in next week's Euro-number and find out.

Psychic News
1992 is knocking on our doors: everywhere poltergeists are preparing for the onslaught and spirits are summoning up their spectral beings. Language is no barrier in the spirit world, neither are walls or doors. Next week: Gubbio and ghosts – a spirit-hunter speaks out; Belgian banshees and French phantoms – a re-appraisal; Gremlins in the Gobelins – the undead of the Uffizi corridors.

The *Sun!*
Wotcha!
1992 – and it's HELLO to hell-raisers across the Channel.

With everything free 'n' easy, Britain can let it all hang out, Continental-style.

Nothing to pay and nothing in the way – as cheeky Cheryl shows us on Page 3. Ooh-la-lady!

The *Financial Times*

1992 marks the completion of the EC internal market, propounded in the SEA of July 1987 and good news for GATT, UCITS, the EEIG and the ECU, although the EMS was starting to falter this week with the latest reports from IDIS.

D. A. PRINCE

Union Jack

To The Editor,
The Times

Dear Sir,

In planning for the understandable celebrations which will take place all over Europe next year, I fear that one most important factor may be overlooked. Our national flag – I refer to the good old Union Jack – is going to be hoisted in a lot of European towns, and in my experience these foreign Johnnies seldom manage to get it the right way up. The consequences, of course, could be disastrous, with any British motorist who happens to be passing dashing into the local Mairie or Stadthuis to try to find the fire that needs putting out or the person who needs rescuing.

May I diffidently put forward my solution to this problem? We should take a leaf out of the book of the chaps who export crates of goods abroad. If we were to amend the flag by the addition of a black umbrella in the centre, it would not only eliminate errors of this type, but also enhance our national standard with a potent symbol of our culture.

Yours faithfully,
Col. G. G. Pharthingale (retd.)

NOEL PETTY

WFNWatson

WHICH Trading Bloc?

Extract from a Consumers Association Special Report

1992 – and trade barriers are down in Europe, for better or worse.

How is the EEC wearing after 25 Years? Is it still good value for money? We looked at its performance, and asked: Is Euro-citizenship still our Best Buy?

The EEC provides adaptable living space, and is easily extended to accommodate a growing family. Starting in 1957 with six living modules, it now has twelve. Surveyors found some ties weaker than we would like (Brussels has yet to concern itself with the standards of ties between countries) 'though the 1960s problem of subsidence in the French corner has largely been overcome.

Although the overall boundary line is untidy – a problem

caused by unco-ordinated bolt-on components – we still liked its flexibility and adaptable profile. But the shape remains a problem: it's not aerodynamic, and no one in our survey could draw an outline map of the EEC. We think Brussels should remedy this and give the EEC a stronger visual identity for consumers: at present consumers identify too closely with their own unit-area (country) and this is a structural weakness that could lead to rusting.

Sadly the EEC is not proving as economical as we'd expected, and the running costs are now prohibitive. A current average of ten tonnes of photo-copier paper per discussion document, and 2002 million expenses-claimed miles per resolution is too high, while housing costs (Brussels and Strasbourg) have risen above inflation levels.

The road-holding qualities of the EEC remain good, but it is slow to corner, often taking several years to negotiate a simple ruling. Speed has never been its top selling point – and zero-to-Single Market in 25 years is not impressive. And while it provides a comfortable ride for bureaucrats in cushioned seats, it offers far less comfort for passengers, particularly in the back seat. It is notoriously lax on child restraint (see *Rod, Pole or a Good Hiding?* Feb., 1990).

Because the EEC has no competitors we feel consumers are deprived of the right to exercise their consumer choice: once locked in to the EEC it is difficult to get out. We'd like the Monopolies Commission to look into this, and especially at some of the more restrictive practices – VAT, for example. But uniformity has advantages – you can now get Diet Coke in Delphi, and Cornettos in Cordova as a result of our recent campaigns.

Does it give value for money? We rocked the boat 6,000 times by putting this question to over 6,000 EEC staff. While we couldn't find anyone to give a firm answer to this question we did learn that a working party of 3,000 economists, and 5,000 support clerical staff (excluding translators) using 2,000 photo-copiers, are currently investigating this issue, and hope to present an interim report in 2002.

D.A. PRINCE

ven in the small country town of Mughampton, every organisation
nd individual is playing a part.

in extract from the minutes of the Europeanisation Sub-Committee
f Mughampton Borough Council, in Room D of the Town Hall.

'HE CHAIRMAN, in his inaugural address, reminded mem-
ers that the Council foresaw vast changes in the British way
f life in 1992. Britain would become more European, and
Mughampton wanted to be in the lead. A large number of
rojects had been suggested, some of which were already
vell under way, and this special committee had been set
up to supervise these, and initiate many more. It was an
xciting brief, and he was proud to have been chosen to
ead the team.

MRS RENÉ HEAVYSIDE asked if his selection had any-
hing to do with his being in the same Masonic Lodge as the
Chairman of the Council, but was ruled out of order.

THE SECRETARY reported upon some of the existing
rojects:

)   The public's response to the introduction of some con-
    tinental dishes to the Meals on Wheels Service was
    disappointing. Several clients had broken their dentures
    on the pizza, and the *escargots* had given rise to a particu-
    larly strong protest. However the Committee would be
    pleased to learn that Meals Assistant Mrs Marcia Palmer
    would be leaving hospital next week. The Meals van was
    off the road at present, for two days, whilst bortsch was
    removed from the petrol tank.

)   Mr Frederick Gudge, owner of 'Fred's Place' on the
    Mughampton By-Pass, had written to say that he had
    been forced to discontinue his Continental Breakfast,
    owing to a lack of interest on the part of his customers in
    the long-distance transport industry. A lorry-driver, 'Big
    Jim' Oakes, was to appear in the Magistrates' Court

Meals on Wheels

next week charged with assault on Mr Gudge and the wilful destruction of 179 bottles of brown sauce and 98 bottles of tomato ketchup. The fire brigade had had to be called to rescue Mr Gudge from the café roof.

c) Mr Rummage had returned from an investigative visit to Denmark with a view to extending the range of magazines and other literature on sale in Mughampton. More samples than anticipated had been obtained, and the necessary extra funds had been despatched to Copenhagen.

COUNCILLOR RUMMAGE said he was grateful for the assistance of an ad hoc reading sub-committee recruited from the Mughampton Rugby Club. An offer of further assistance from the ladies of the WI had been turned down, as the present sub-committee had more than enough volunteers.

THE MUGHAMPTON OPERA HOUSE PROJECT

THE CHAIRMAN said that this was the most ambitious project to date, but the Council had become aware that many continental cities of any consequence had at least one Opera House, and Mughampton could not allow itself to remain a cultural desert. Councillors Mrs Lydia Bellows and Mr Jolyon Jollyboy were even now on a fact-finding tour of Europe. At present they were in Salzburg, and intended travelling on to Vienna, Milan and Monte Carlo, where, it was understood, there might be opera houses for them to visit.

E.O. PARROTT

From the Mughampton Sun

MARBLES MISHAP

Mughampton's marbles team failed to play its scheduled fixture at Chaton-sur-Mer because its marbles went missing. The players, in the charge of Euro-trotting Councillor Jolyon Jollyboy, were said to be 'in high spirits' at the ship's bar on the crossing to France, and during some heavy horse-play the star player, Reg Froth, had his trousers pulled off. When he got them back the team's marbles, which had been in his pocket, could not be found. On arrival at Chaton the team was offered substitute *billes* to play with, but declined on the ground that these might have been 'doctored'. This accusation infuriated the Frenchmen, and the Mughamptonians beat an ignominious retreat. On their return home, Councillor Nathaniel Muffin, who had refused to go on the trip said: 'I could have told those Frogs at the start that this lot had lost their marbles anyway.'

PETER VEALE

Mughampton Gnome Works Staff Committee

Minutes Of Extraordinary Meeting Of Sub-Committee On 'Project Europe'

Present:
J.B. Clatworthy – General Manager (Chairman)
F.H.C. Harcourt-Jones – Marketing
Miss J.W. Johnson – Design
P.K. Prodwind – Production
F.P. Smoothie – Personnel
F. Tonks – Paint Shop Convener
Mrs S. Wilkinson – Secretary

1. Introduction
Mr Clatworthy welcomed everyone to the first meeting of the sub-committee. He made no apology for starting with a short speech to stress the need for the sub-committee to exercise real vision, to raise its sights above the mundane matters which had sometimes bogged down the Works Committee in the past. The task before the sub-committee now was part of the historic mission to weld together a great continent, and Little Mughampton Gnome Works should not be found wanting.

2. Administrative Matters
Mr Tonks pointed out that in the Works Committee minutes which had set up the sub-committee his name had appeared after that of the Secretary, who was not in fact a full member of the sub-committee, but only an observer and reporter. Mr Clatworthy regretted the oversight. It was agreed that the correct sequence of names should be that of the Chairman, followed by the full members in alphabetical order, followed by the Secretary.

3. Europization
The Chairman outlined the history of the Company, which, though illustrious, had hitherto been confined to its native shores. The opportunity of Europe was now wide open,

and he invited those present to start the proceedings with a brainstorm on how the Company's product range might be Europized for 1992.

After a false start, it was explained by Mr Smoothie to Mr Tonks that it was implicit in the idea of a brainstorm that laughter at other members' suggestions was inhibiting to the creative process. Mr Tonks promptly apologised to Mr Prodwind and the session resumed, yielding the following ideas for further evaluation and scrutiny:

Germany

Mr Harcourt-Jones expressed the view that little modification would be required for the German market, since garden gnomes were culturally based on Bavarian traditions anyway. He cited the legend of Snow White and the Seven Dwarfs in support, which led to a brief reminiscence of his childhood by Mr Clatworthy. Mr Tonks' suggestion of the addition of a small toothbrush moustache was thought not to be in the spirit of 1992.

France

A Gallic gnome was not thought to present too much of a problem. Miss Johnson believed that a modification of the mould to flatten the peaked hat into beret form would be quite feasible, and Mr Tonks said that the Paint Shop's resources were up to the job of a striped sweater. There was some doubt about whether Mr Prodwind's idea of placing a small frog under the toadstool would be received in a properly good-humoured spirit, and Mr Harcourt-Jones undertook to do additional market research in the area of French humour.

Spain

Miss Johnson's idea of using the cultural icon of a matador was welcomed enthusiatically. The addition of a cape would be no problem, and the gnome's tunic and trousers could be painted as a multi-coloured 'suit of lights'. Mr Tonks expressed severe reservations about the demands that this would place on the Paint Shop, but agreed that resistance might be overcome by a new agreement on overtime rates and skill-related payments. Miss Wikinson intervened at this point, saying that as an animal rights supporter and vegetarian she could not condone the use of this symbol. Mr Tonks then asked, on a point of order, whether Miss Wilkinson was entitled to express an opinion. Mr Smoothie explained to Mr Tonks that, since ideas only were being expressed, Miss Wilkinson's contribution should be accepted, and to Miss Wilkinson that no action would be taken without full consideration of the sensibilities of employees.

Portugal

This was acknowledged to be a difficult one. The only lead which was produced came from Mr Clatworthy, who reminisced about an aunt of his who had been stung by a Portuguese Man of War while bathing at Westcliff-on-Sea. Miss Johnson expressed doubt about the feasibility of converting the familiar mould quite so radically as to produce a convincing replica of a jelly-fish, and Mr Harcourt-Jones was not hopeful of a ready acceptance of such a product in Portuguese markets. He was not sure whether the Portuguese accepted ownership of this species; as he put it: 'For all we know they may call the things English Men of War over there.' Further research was called for.

Denmark

The initial idea of simply painting the gnomes to resemble Danish Blue cheese was thought unappealing. However, the Hans Anderson connection was thought to have considerably more potential, gnomes not being readily distinguishable from trolls, goblins etc. At a pinch, therefore, it was agreed that the existing models would serve very well. A suggestion from Mr Prodwind that the mould be modified to incorporate something which he swore he had seen on open display on news stands and novelty shops in Copenhagen was hastily terminated by Mr Clatworthy, who agreed that Mr Prodwind could go into detail on another occasion when certain members of the sub-committee were not present. It was, however, unlikely to be adopted.

Greece

No overpowering image of Greek connection thrust itself forward. Mr Harcourt-Jones, however, recalled from his military days that the Greek soldiers, when in full dress for guards of honour, were in the habit of wearing a kind of wide white skirt, with a sort of tasselled cap not unlike that worn by the standard gnome. This in turn prompted Miss Johnson to remember the Scottish campaign of 1962, when a new mould was made of a gnome wearing a kilt and playing bagpipes; she believed the mould was still in a store cupboard. The campaign had foundered on the difficulty the Paint Shop had with tartan, but of course that question would not now arise. Mr Clatworthy expressed great gratification at this juxtaposition of ideas, since this was exactly how brain storming ought to work. Mr Harcourt-Jones undertook to find out what a bouzouki was, and check on its bagpipe-convertibility.

Ireland

It was generally agreed that Ireland would present no difficulty; the existing gnomes would simply be painted green and make very presentable leprechauns. Mr Clatworthy expressed a view that the addition of a clay pipe held upside down would enhance the attractiveness of the figure further; but after listening to Miss Wilkinson's objection about the discouragement of smoking and Mr Prodwind's warning about the fragility of small projections in plaster figures, conceded the point.

Belgium

Several members of the sub-committee had visited Brussels, and all seemed to recall one symbol in particular, that of a well-known statue of a small boy in the act of relieving himself. Mr Clatworthy said that this was a very delicate area, and the Company must be mindful of its reputation. We lived in liberated times, it was true, but that section of the public which formed the prime buying-group for the garden gnome was not necessarily ready for this kind of thing. Miss Wilkinson, to some members' surprise, expressed the view that there was nothing to be ashamed of in the display of a natural bodily function. Encouraged by this view, Mr Clatworthy gave the go-ahead for 'Project Le Gnome Pis'.

Luxembourg

No member of the sub-comittee could recall meeting a Luxembourger. Mr Harcourt-Jones, however, asserted that Luxembourg used to have a Grand-Duke and very possibly still had. Until anything more inspiring came forward, therefore, Miss Johnson was authorised to proceed with designs incorporating a Ducal crown into the Gnomal hat.

The Netherlands

Miss Johnson said that Dutch traditional dress would not present major difficulties. The standard gnome already had sizable feet, due she believed to the influence of the late Miss Enid Blyton and her protégé, Noddy. The conversion to clogs would therefore be relatively simple, and baggy trousers would complete the picture. A suggestion that the toadstool be converted to a windmill was made by the tea-lady, Mrs Grommet, who happened to be present, but the problems of execution in this case were thought to be more severe. At Mr Clatworthy's request, Mr Prodwind's offer to describe a number of objects he had seen during a recent visit to Amsterdam was adjourned *sine die* in view of the limited time available.

Italy

Mr Harcourt-Jones wasn't sure whether the Italians went in for gardens very much, but proposed wrapping the gnome in a toga. Although superficially attractive, the idea was thought to be insufficiently modern for the spirit of 1992. An alternative suggestion of a papal crown was also rejected both for the same reason and because of Mr Smoothie's fears of possible charges of insensitivity. The most appealing idea was that of setting the gnome on a scooter of the Lambretta type, which Mr Harcourt-Jones believed still flourished in the Italian cities. The idea was enthusiastically supported by all members except Miss Johnson, who had reservations about the design problems.

Summary

Mr Clatworthy thanked everyone for the remarkable flow of ideas which he had witnessed. He recalled the time when his father had founded the factory, fifty years ago. Little had he thought then of the glittering international future that was now opening up. He was expanding on this theme when several members of the sub-committee remembered urgent appointments and the meeting was adjourned.

NOEL PETTY

Language Teaching – A Protest

To: The Editor
The *Mughampton Sun*

Dear Sir,

I am concerned about recent developments in the teaching of languages in our schools.

Whilst I am not against a certain amount of language tuition as part of a child's education, I learn with horror that my daughter, who is taking her GCSE at Mughampton Upper School, has been asked if she would like to do an exchange visit with a French girl, spending three months living with a French family, in France, where she would be expected to speak French all the time.

So far as I am aware, the teaching of French at school was never intended to prepare people for speaking the language. Of course, a knowledge of catering terms in French can come in useful in some restaurants, and when travelling in France one should be able to hold one's own with waiters, ticket collectors, gendarmes, and other such persons. But all educated French people speak English, and surely, they are the only ones a really nice girl need spend her time talking to.

As English people, we ought to be proud of our magnificent language, and continue to use it everywhere we can. Going into Europe should not mean a lowering of our standards, or 'going native'.

Yours etc.,
Gladys Muffin (Mrs)

E.O. PARROTT

To: The Editor,
The *Mughampton Sun*

Dear Sir,

I want to disagree most strongly with your recent correspondent who claims that you can't get a decent cup of tea anywhere on the continent.

Last year my husband and I went on a coach holiday for the over 60s to five European countries in eight days. Or it might have been eight European countries in five days. My memory is not what it was. About the third day we stopped for toilets on the E15 (why do they call all their roads after additives?) between Hamburg and Hanover and saw a Robin Reliant just like the one we used to own which was stolen. You hear a lot about cars being thieved in England and sold abroad so we asked the driver who was under the bonnet where he had bought it. He told us he got it through the *Exchange & Mart* from a man in Chislehurst so that was alright. Anyway, the driver who turned out to be a Mr Wheeler had a gadget which he plugged into the cigarette lighter in his dashboard and dangled the twirly bit on the other end into a teapot. We were soon all enjoying a good strong cup of Brooke Bond Divi.

So you can get a good cuppa in Europe after all. Mr Wheeler says he goes motoring on the continent every year so readers who like a good cup of Rosie Lee should look out for him. Apparently he spends a lot of time brewing up in car parks waiting for Europ Assist.

Yours faithfully,
Gladys Small (Mrs)

V. ERNEST COX

. . . good strong cup of Brooke Bond Divi . . .

Mughampton Women's Institute

From the minutes of the Sub-Committee for Europeanization:

Mrs Heavyside reported on the 'Beautiful Mughampton' campaign. She and other members had been to Switzerland on a week's tour, and had been impressed by Swiss standards of cleanliness. They were determined to make Mughampton as neat and pretty as Basle or Lausanne, and would stop at nothing to achieve this aim. Each member would be responsible for galvanizing her immediate circle into action:

1. Mrs Amalia Trench and the Mughampton Horticultural Society were undertaking floral decorations and, with the aid of a Council grant, proposed to line the streets with tubs of flowers, bulbs and shrubs, and to strike an original note, unusual receptacles were being sought. Mr Fred Boot had offered an old hip bath which he had recovered from the canal, and old Joshua Boot had turned

up trumps with an original Victorian pig trough – a real find, Mrs Trench had said.

2. Mrs Doreen Stillworthy had persuaded Messrs KLEEN-ABRIX to donate a quantity of their product for cleaning pavements, walls and front steps, and this had already been distributed to all except the inhabitants of Guy Lane, who had refused point blank to use it as they said it would destroy the many unique pieces of mural and pavement art with which this area abounds.

3. The Art Department of Mughampton College of Further Education, together with High Street shopkeepers, were designing banners with symbols denoting the various trades and professions, under the Arms of Mughampton. This was still at the drawing-board stage.

4. Mrs Ruddle had been asked to approach Mr Ruddle with a view to cleaning up the Station. He had admitted that it was a bit grubby, but he did not want to upset old Mr Porter, the porter, as he was getting on now, and tended to wait for a strong wind to blow the dust away. Mrs Ruddle had said she would persevere with this.

E. O. PARROTT

More from the Mughampton Sun

SHOVE OFF

An attempt to restore Mughampton's sporting reputation in the French resort of Chaton-sur-Mer has ended in failure. A shove-ha'penny team from the Tattooed Arms arrived in Chaton ready to play the locals; but before the board could be set up at a seafront hotel, a European monetary official dramatically appeared. He declared that the contest would be illegal, since it involved a coin which had not been in use for some years and would never again be part of European currency. Both teams angrily pointed out that the game was played with counters, not actual halfpennies. But the bureaucrat insisted that the law was clear. Anglo-French accord was established when both teams attacked the official. Baton-wielding gendarmes finally restored order. No charges were made against the Mughampton men, but they were put on the boat for home.

PETER VEALE

Report On The 'Ooh La La! Mein Signor, Por Favor' Competition at Mughampton's Safegate Supermarket

Competitors for our prize of a weekend for two in Gay Paree were asked to identify the nationality of typical Europeans in pictures printed on the labels of our own-brand toilet paper. To decide between all-correct entries, the tie-breaker was to write not more than ten words beginning, 'I fancy a weekend in Gay Paree because . . .'.

First, the pictures. The gentleman in the spangled suit waving his cape at a charging bull was from . . . yes, sunny Spain! An impressive 30% of you got this one right, though I sympathise with those who thought he was from India, where these animals are also held in high regard. Next, the girl with the ice cream standing in front of the leaning building. A tricky one this – some of you thought it was from Japan after an earthquake, but remember, it's still in Europe. Over 20% guessed correctly that she was Italian. Then the jolly fellow in the clogs with the windmill behind. No, he wasn't from Oldham, he was a Dutchman, or I'm a Dutchman. Get it? Well, 19% of you did. And finally a really tough one, the gent in the beret and hooped shirt with the onions round his neck. Some of you thought they were swedes and went for our Scandinavian friends, but the right answer, which 15% of you got, was French. The object behind him was meant to be a clue, but some people thought it was Blackpool Tower and got confused. Sorry about that.

So to the tie-breaker. First our apologies both to the gay community, who threatened us with the Advertising Standards Authority when it transpired that the prize was a straight weekend; and also to the Citizens' Vigilante Group, who thought just the opposite. Honestly, don't blame us, we're not in charge of the English language. Also, we should have made it clear that the partner in the 'weekend for two' would have to be supplied by the winner.

We were puzzled, too, by the entry which read, '. . . because it makes the cow so happy,' but we finally worked out that the entrant had got confused between this one and last week's one on our milk ('I always drink Safegate's Milk because . . . it has that spicy continental flavour.'). After disqualifying a few for sending in identical entries, we gave the second prize (a fresh baguette) to Mr Mayling, for his telling '. . . because Safegate is an excellent company on which one can rely in every way', but felt it didn't quite have the precise appositeness required to win the prize. So the weekend goes to our overall winner, who, somewhat disappointingly, asked to remain anonymous and to have the tickets sent in a plain brown envelope. The winning line was, '. . . because an "eiffel" of the girls there keeps me "seine".' Congratulations, Mr Polewheel!

NOEL PETTY

The Chunnel for Mughampton

To: The Editor,
Mughampton Echo

Dear Sir,

We are continually reading in our newspapers, and seeing on television, reports about the difficulties experienced by the Channel Tunnel Company in finding a suitable place for a terminal on the British side of the Channel. The people of Kent seem to be very selfish. Does not this, however, represent a wonderful opportunity for Mughampton to show its European spirit and offer itself for this purpose? It is surely not too late to extend the tunnel from Dover to the old South Mughampton gravel pits, where the excavations already made would be a good start. And how wonderful it would be for our Continental friends to emerge from their journey in the heart of England's Green and Pleasant Land, to a nice welcoming cuppa at Mrs Bastable's Tea Rooms!

Yours, etc.

P. Wickens (Miss)

Our transport correspondent writes:
Full marks for creative thinking, Miss Wickens, and the warm-heartedness of your sentiments does you credit. I have mentioned your idea to the Channel Tunnel Company, but they rather feel that Mughampton, situated as it is some ninety miles from the coast, would present them with a number of difficulties which could not be easily overcome. As you may know, they are working to a rather tight budget. They did pause in their labours, however, to ask me to convey their warmest thanks for your thought.

NOEL PETTY

Your Questions Answered

Q. What is Britain most famous in Europe for producing?
Britain has always been famous for its coal, ship-building, oil and tourist industries, although times do change, and new industries spring up all the time. Only a few years ago, for instance, the 'burgher' was a dish which was exported from Calais – as those of you with GCSE History will know. But now Scotland has taken over the making of this popular dish, which it sells as a **Big Mac**, after its maker, the former cider-farmer, **Apple Mackintosh**. The Big Mackintosh, unlike its French cousin, is designed for indoors. Britain currently exports more tourists than anyone else, but we are looking to redress this balance in time for the opening of the Channel Tunnel (or **Chanel Tunnel**, as the French call it, after its major sponsor). At present Britain is therefore engaged in building hundreds of holiday houses in rural England and Wales, all white, thatched, and with roses round the door: the so-called **'cottage industry'**.

The Burgers of Calais

Q. What do the other countries in the EEC make?
Eire produces peat, and also bogs (I'm afraid that they
were first to invent them, long before **Looe** and **Flushing**, who also claim to be the original manufacturers).

. . . before Looe or Flushing.

France is famous for its **pâtisserie** (pastry), **pharmacie**
(agriculture), **boutiques** (cobblers) and **magazins** (literature). Italy makes pasta, the main ingredient in Cornish
pasties and the drink 'pastis' amongst other things. It
also makes **spaghetti, ravioli, zucchini** and **deli**, the spicy
and rather peculiar food you can buy at special shops
throughout the continent. Greece produces olives, with
or without stones, and sometimes in a hybrid form with
red pepper. It is thereby also the chief oil producer in
the Common Market, and the Community's chief rep-
resentative in OPEC. Portugal manufactures **algarve**, a
famous cloth, not unlike linen. Denmark is best known
for its butter, its bacon and its enormous dogs (bred to
be mountain rescuers in the Swiss resort of St Bernard).
Belgium produces two national commodities – **phlegm**,
a gluey substance, and **walloons**, which are like balloons,
only bigger. Holland makes Lego, although it is also
known for its light industry, manufacturing hundreds

Denmark is best known for its
butter, bacon and enormous dogs . . .

of bulbs. Germany makes **Frankfurters** and **Hamburgers**
and mattresses (**Vorsprung**). Spain is known throughout
Europe for its television, which is beamed all over the
EEC from its headquarters in Granada. For many years,
the monarchists overthrown by Franco produced the
programme which I am told Britons know as *Coronation
Street* from an illegal broadcasting station, never discovered by the Generalissimo. And Luxembourg is famous
for its **radio**, and its special 'white noise' touch of
authenticity.

Q. Where did the duvet come from?
Bedfordshire. It replaced the Scandinavian ice-sheet.

BILL GREENWELL

EUROBRITS

We have been concentrating our attention in this book largely on Continental Europe as seen by the British Europhile. But how should he see himself? This chapter offers a brief guide.

The British

Oh, no-one hates being British like the British.
Take your liberal, educated Brit.
His heart is sadly torn, that the fact of being born,
In this island guarantees he'll be a shit.
His hatred of his nationhood's deep-seated,
He throws up when he sees his flag unfurled;
Oh no-one hates being British like the liberal British –
We're the worst bloody country in the world.

This trait is not in-bred in Anglo-Saxons.
Americans will boast of being Yanks,
And if you mistake Canadians for being anything but
   Canadian,
They are the last to give you any thanks.
New Zealanders quite relish being New Zealanders.
Australians, God knows why, are pretty proud
Of their suburban trim to the outback's rim –
At least they tell you so, and very loud.

But those who got their ancestors exported,
Through poverty or penal servitude,
Find an antipathy in being what they're forced to be,
And on the subject of their origins, are rude.

... ancestors exported ...

And they scrutinise their character to pieces,
And on themselves, they practice Cultural Crit.
Oh no-one hates being British like the British hate being
  British.
Your liberal, educated, travelled Brit.

Italians dance and sing at being Italian,
French savants endure being very French,
Being Swiss is total bliss to the average Swiss,
Being Danish doesn't cause the Danes to blench,
But take your open-minded, thinking British;
On themselves, they'll call down every curse.
We're utterly obscene, lowest that's ever been.
No-one else could ever have been worse.

Belgians are quite happy being Belgian,
Swedes aren't ashamed to say that they are Swedes,
Spaniards think they've made a gain in being citizens
  of Spain,
Poles think the Poles the finest of all breeds.

Germans have got used to being German,
They're living down their recent past, a bit,
But for a drench of guilt that would make a forest
wilt,
Go to your liberal-minded Brit.

The middle-class, *Guardian*-reading Briton,
Likes abusing his own country best.
Americans are more open and much more freely
    spoken;
Italians are surely better dressed.
The Greeks are nicer, friendlier and kinder;
The Irish have much the greater charm;
For tolerance and such, we're beaten by the Dutch;
Greenlanders have done the world less harm.

Iceland has much the nicer weather;
Russians don't keep trains in such a fug;
Yes, the whole world's full of hate for the British state,
We're one and all so bloody pleased and smug.
At outdoor cafes you will often find them,
World-Service listening, with exported beer:
'The country would not alter, so now I live in Malta
I find them much less insular right here.'

'I tell you,' they say, tearful and vehement,
'We're passionless, superior and cold.'
Yes, the sun never sets, on where a Briton frets,
How awful his country was of old,
How horrible it was to have an empire,
How pathetic, to have an empire lost,
How only the short-sighted are by Europe undelighted,
When for so long they have been US-bossed.

Oh no-one hates being British like the British,
A cosmopolitan Briton, you can trust,
To rate his television, with snorts of deep derision,
And constantly he's full of self-disgust.
Oh no-one hates being British like the British;

Our country, it really is the pits.
Our police always unlawful, our food so bloody awful.
No-one hates being British like the Brits.

REM BEL

Left Behind Blues

So, mum, you're on the Costa Brava!
(You might as well have gone to Java)
Thank you for your note: 'I've gone.
Leave the central heating on.
Help yourself to gin and It:
I think I've left a tiny bit.'
As always, you're above all mothers
In your tender care for others.

Come back, mum, and bring with you
Bottles of that Spanish brew.
I know my words aren't any use:
You've the necessary juice
Where you are; and you'll be wise
To stay until the swallow flies.
Swallow? Swallow, did I say?
So I will, if that's the way.

If I could only find by art
Some Costa Brava of the heart,
Transcendental Meditation
Might ease my urge for emigration.
As it is, Mum, since you're there
And I can't afford the fare,
I'll give the gin another go –
Winter's hard in Walthamstow.

PAUL GRIFFIN

A Short Guide To British Towns

Bath

A city founded by the Romans who were obsessed with cleanliness. It was brought into prominence in the 18th century by an influx of beaux, initiated by a member of the local constabulary, PC Wren, who introduced Beau Geste into the area. Others included Beau Brunel who invented a card game called Iron Bridge, and Beau Ogden Nash who designed the Pump Room, a favourite stopping place for motorists.

Beaux play Iron Bridge in Bath

Birmingham

This has many surprising features including Bournville, a village constructed entirely out of chocolate, and a hazardous road junction made of pasta.

Cambridge

A university centre associated with many famous people, including Francis Bacon, who always insisted that his name was Shakespeare, and Isaac Walton who made the momentous discovery that if you let go of an apple it will hit the floor.

Canterbury

Noted for three things: bells, lamb and tales. The origin of the tales springs from a priest, Samuel Beckett who habitually loitered in the cathedral. When asked the reason for this he turbulently replied, 'Oh, I'm waiting for God.' Henry II, who could not stand turbulence, had him martyred. About two hundred years later a tour operator, Cheerful Charlie Chaucer (who was notoriously bad at spelling) organised trips from London to Canterbury. The tales (which are of a salacious nature) were told to while away the time in traffic hold-ups on the A2.

Cardiff

This is the capital of Wales and its most hallowed building is a pub, 'The Cardiff Arms'.

Coventry

Considering the number of people who have been forcibly sent there over the years its population is not as large as one might imagine. It has never completely recovered from the famous ride taken by Lady Godiva who constantly refused to visit a hairdresser. When asked the reason for this she replied 'I've got something to hide'; a remark that has puzzled scholars for centuries.

Edinburgh

A beautiful city known affectionately as 'Auld Cock-a-Leekie', the home of the kilt, sporran and haggis. A notable thoroughfare is the Royal Smile, named in honour of the Duke of Edinburgh. Film lovers should not miss Hollywood House which was once the home of James Stewart.

Glasgow

An impressive place with a tendency to revolve on Saturday nights.

Liverpool

For many years it had a tenuous association with shipping, but it was not until the sixties that it suddenly sprang to fame when it was subjected to a plague of beetles. These insects became so much a part of the lives of the inhabitants that they grew resigned to them and even gave them affectionate names: Jack Lemmon, Rex Harrison, Charlie McCarthy and Harpo Marx.

London

The Tower of London is a medieval fortress where, for hundreds of years, the sovereign had awkward politicians beheaded. There is at the present time, a strong movement to revive this practice.

St Paul's Cathedral was designed by Sir Christopher Robin who always insisted on complete silence when he said his prayers there.

Westminster Abbey has inspired more than one poet to remark on the number of tombs it contains. These apparently embody the remains of those Londoners who, according to Dr Johnson, got tired of living there.

Piccadilly Circus is dominated by a statue of the god, Enos, which symbolises the country's tradition with the salty ocean surrounding it. Along with Leicester Square, Piccadilly is a useful jumping-off place for those wishing to visit Tipperary, but be warned: it's a long way.

Newcastle

The foreign visitor must be prepared for the revelation that an English dictionary is of little use in these parts. The two most noted names here are Geordie and his wife, Hinny, to whom constant reference is made. Newcastle is close to Hadrian's Wall, which was built by an over-optimistic Roman Emperor to stop the Scots coming into England – a project that was doomed to utter failure.

Oxford

It would take up far too much space to enumerate all the famous and learned people connected with this beautiful city, but one worthy of note is the dancing pioneer, William Morris, who is even better known through his younger brother, Morris minor, and his daughter, Minnie.

FRANK RICHARDS

Conversation Pieces

Why do the British keep Royals?
They're priced beyond valuation.
They're useful objects to their subjects,
By being subjects of conversation.
When the hassle of living in London falters,
And the state of the roads and the rails,
There's always the corpulent Duchess of York,
The filiform Princess of Wales.

The British talk about gardening.
Though now herbs in patio pots,
Replace the failures of their dahlias,
And the clay in those long narrow plots.
But how to trellis the walls can pall,
And setting of slug traps slump;
Then the Princess of Wales is a mad anorexic,
The Duchess, pleasantly plump.

A Briton's never a slave of course,
But he's his Bank Manager's liege,
The Briton's a vassal in a mortgaged castle,
Which high interest rates besiege.
So when he starts on how the price he paid's doubled,
Or how he's tied to a subsiding dump,
Contend that the Princess is sexily svelte,
The Duchess, an overgrown lump.

The British have always gone travelling,
The rich, to avoid paying tax,
The poor go on an all-paid-package,
In order to get pissed in packs.
You will see both classes queueing at kiosks,
Buying tabloids in Jersey and Greece,
For the latest on the Princess' diet,
And what makes the Duchess obese.

Could Britain ever be a Republic?
What interest could anyone find,
In a Mrs Wales's slender hips,
And Sarah York's big behind.
Meat for discussion, already on ration,
At the office, in pubs and clubs fails,
Without the fat on the Duchess of York,
The lean on the Princess of Wales.

REM BEL

EUROWARNINGS

How To Remain Completely Unaffected By Abroad

When in **Amsterdam**

Do NOT visit the red light district. Its alliance between lust, commercialism and cosy domesticity (crudely shouting or furtively sidling men assessing naked girls knitting behind lace curtains in comfy front rooms) may induce disturbing reflections on sexuality and social mores.

Do NOT go anywhere near the canals. You will be bitten by midges.

When in **Cardiff**

Do NOT attend a rugby match at the Welsh National Stadium. It is always best to tread carefully when fundamentalist religion is on the agenda. Welsh crowds know in their deepest hearts that their national side is never fairly beaten. Sometimes, through cheating and the incompetence of a referee appointed from the ranks of the aurally and visually handicapped, a visiting team may be awarded more points, but such mishaps should not be thought of as a Welsh defeat. The outsider, by definition impartial and measured in judgement, will keep all comment to himself. Indeed, if he retains the wit he was born with, he will cheer loudly in the Welsh interest. Should impartiality preclude this subterfuge, he will make an excuse, *pianissimo*, and leave. Even so, he may be pursued by small swarthy men, who will belabour him with muddy-rooted leeks and shout abuse rendered almost musical by its unparalleled liquidity

of vowel. Indeed, if matters really do come to a head they may
burst into unaccompanied choral song, which is worse.

When in **Castiglione del Lago**

DO NOT travel to the islands of the lake, where the Rosemary
is six feet high, abandoned chapels and castles are redolent
of people and times unknown, and jolly Italians picnic and
dance dappled by shadows in the olive groves. You will be
bitten by midges.

When in **Copenhagen**

DO NOT ride the Big Dipper in the Tivoli Gardens. To be flung
spear-like to within inches of a solid wall, to be snatched
away in an Immelman turn; to climb and plummet vertically
within one breathless, terrified giggle; to cling to a retaining
bar, your torso parallel to the solid, blurred Danish earth
which hurtles past inches below in horizontal parallel: these

are experiences to test the most sanguine of men. Danish sadism (remember the rape and pillage which accompanied their visits to our own peaceable land!) is such that you are mad to endure them twice.

Do NOT make a pilgrimage to the Little Mermaid. This tiny, isolated statue, pensive on its plinth in the sea, its back turned on the ferries and their mournful lowing as they leave for Malmo, is a melancholy work, inspired by a fairy tale of Hans Christian Andersen, whose morbidly acute personality did not remotely resemble the avuncular zany portrayed by Danny Kaye in the eponymous film. In some seasons of the year it may be warm enough for you to be bitten by midges.

When in **Edinburgh**

Do NOT visit the castle on a fine afternoon in August hoping to catch a sundrenched panorama of the stern romantic city. Let stained, hill-clutching Old Town buildings straggle down Canongate to Holyrood; let New Town stand serene in its Georgian order beyond Princes Street: in the minutes it takes to achieve your coign of vantage, a thick, concealing mist, will fall, clinging to buildings and people, penetrating the stoutest, warmest facade. You might as well be in Glencoe in February, so muffled and so sinister is the scene. A piper tuning up in some invisible courtyard below is all you need to complete your saturation in that Caledonian mysticism which comes so readily to the Athens of the North.

When in **Konstanze**

Do NOT stroll by the lake or along the blue peaceful Rhine. You will be bitten by German midges. And there are too many tulips, to say nothing of the cabbages.

When in **Madrid**

Do NOT lunch at L'Hardy's downstairs. There is nowhere to sit while you browse on the *tapas* (olives, tiny fritters and meatballs) and sluice on the endless sherries, madeiras and manzanillos which are available for the London price of a slice of sticky pizza.

Do NOT dine at Botin's. Someone there will be wondering which was Hemingway's favourite table. The roast sucking pig (*cochinillo asado* – be warned) is addictive. And wine at under a pound a bottle is very bad for you.

When in **Naples**
Do NOT visit Pompeii. Some guides will prevent your wife or other female companion from seeing the naughty statues and paintings and you will be subjected to a feminist tirade for the rest of the day.

. . . some guides will prevent your wife
or other female companion from seeing . . .

When in **Oban**
You will be bitten by midges.

When in **Paris**
Do NOT visit the Louvre. Crowds of ignoramuses, who block your view of the paintings – especially the Mona Lisa, which, to make matters worse, does its simpering within an Eichmannite protective glass booth. The collection at large consists principally of works by artists who were French or lived at some time in France. It has, therefore, only parochial interest.

Do NOT walk on the banks of the Seine. You may see topless sunbathers, or variously paired lovers engaging in acts better confined between four walls, if attempted at all. There are odours of exotic foods and even more exotic cigarettes. If you don't smoke yourself you will be bitten by midges.

DO NOT walk up the Rue St Denis. Ingenious arrangements of buckles and straps, the working gear of the young women – some not so young! – who ply their trade there, will induce troubled ponderings on the follies of mankind. Worse, any inadvertently over-attentive gaze will be construed as the go-ahead for commercial negotiations.

DO NOT go anywhere near, let alone up the Eiffel Tower. When it was first built, Parisian intellectuals took troublesome and lengthy detours to avoid seeing it. Today their eyes-off stance remains the only only one possible to those who care for architectural sense and decorum. The thing lacks human scale, is visually out of sympathy with its surroundings and is constructed in soulless iron.

DO NOT eat casserole of guinea fowl and drink *vin ouvert* in a cheap Seine-side restaurant. You might go native, raise your glass to dull care and engage vivaciously in wide-ranging philosophical debate without so much as a stammer of British reticence.

DO NOT travel on the Métro. You will infallibly get lost and arrive late. It is not because the system is unclearly arranged or badly sign-posted, nor because trains are irregular or infrequent. *Au contraire*: the welcoming Art Nouveau entrances, the wide, airy, uncrowded platforms, the clean, elegantly curving tiled walls and the apt decorative displays at individual stations all combine to induce a disorientating feeling that you are not in a transport system at all. Rather, you have found a spot for withdrawal, a place of meditation, detached from the bustling purposefulness of the city a few feet above your head.

DO NOT visit Montmartre. You have seen it all already in reproductions of impressionist paintings.

DO NOT visit the Gare d'Orsay. To have so much of the art of the nineteenth century under one (high, glazed) roof is to risk indigestion of the senses.

DO NOT visit Versailles. The absurd, pretentious architecture will make you feel that the French Revolution was necessary, and this has become an unfashionable view.

When in **Switzerland**

DO NOT venture into the streets. Their spotlessness will make you feel grimy.

When in **Vienna**

DO NOT look for the beautiful blue Danube. What you will find is brownish and non-descript. You will be bitten by midges.

DO NOT walk around the Ringstrasse exclaiming delightedly at the variety of architectural periods exemplified by the buildings. They are all fakes, run up in the mid-nineteenth century.

DO NOT eat potatoes made of marzipan or elephants made of meringue. The idea is kitsch and disgusting.

DO NOT visit Grinzing to drink the new season's wine in the lively backyards of the *heurigen*. The wine tastes innocuously delicious and comes in half pint mugs. You may get drunk and start to sing. Besides, the waitresses wear laced, extrusive bodices, rendering the entire enterprise replete with moral risk. And you will be bitten by midges.

DO NOT lift up sewer covers hoping to hear mysterious echoes of Harry Lime's zither or see the orotund ghost of Orson Welles. Police will blow whistles at you.

DO NOT ride on the big wheel in the Prater. Orson Welles isn't up there either and the view is of a railway marshalling yard.

DO NOT listen to small groups of men in green jackets and with feathers in their hat bands playing valveless horns. Their repertoire of fanfares will put you in mind of hunting, fighting and other unacceptable pursuits.

DO NOT gaze at shop windows displaying candles or hats.

In Grinzing . . . enterprise replete with moral risk . . .

Either will induce gloomy, envious meditations on the evils of conspicuous consumption.

Do NOT shop in the Flea Market. You will infallibly buy something you could have got more cheaply at home.

Do NOT go to see the Klimts and Schieles in the Belvedere Palace. They are erotic and disturbing.

Do NOT walk on any paving stone which looks more than forty years old. It may have been hewn by slave labour in Mauthausen, the death camp up the river.

When in Venice

Do NOT ride in a gondola. You will be ripped off and may have to endure songs rendered fortissimo, in Italian, a few feet above your head. You will be bitten by midges.

Do NOT go to the Scuola di San Rocco to see the cycle of Tintoretto's paintings on the life of Christ. Even on hot days the building is cool. In winter you may actually shiver. To preserve them the paintings are ill lit. They hang high on the walls. A clearer, less neck-ricking perusal is obtainable in any of the books of reproductions which are available at reasonable cost.

Do NOT eat the ice cream. It is not manufactured to British standards and there is a worrying possibility that you might enjoy it exceedingly.

Do NOT eat uncooked salads. They may contain dandelion leaves and other perils too horrific to list in a publication designed for the nervous. See also above, under warnings about ice cream.

Do NOT drink coffee at Florian's or Quadri's in the Piazza San Marco. An extortionate bill is the least of the competing perils. Paunchy, exclamatory Americans, shutter-rattling, miya-samaing Japanese, otiose, lumbering Germans and vehement, gesticulating Italians gabble in their various patois. Chairs scrape on the pavement. Crockery clatters on metal tables. The bands of the two establishments overlap:

The Barber of Seville counterpointing 'Yes, Sir, That's My Baby'. Chimes thunder from the towering campanile. Gobbling pigeons and screeching gulls wheel and mass, their curving kamikaze dives targetting any unattended foody fragment. The flicker and rustle of wings is a background susurration, growing at intervals to a pulsing rush which obliterates all other sounds. Guides, rallying straggled parties, wave brightly coloured umbrellas, clap their hands and utter undecodable cries. Add to all these auditory and visual stimulations the whispering ghosts of a millenium of political and social turbulence and you will be lucky to escape without a severe headache. This may be the world's drawing room, but the guests are ill-matched, clamorous and too many.

DO NOT visit San Francesco del Deserto. You have to travel first to the island of Burano, where, amongst the variegated cottages of the fisherfolk, the main street features a communist headquarters. Then you must hang about on the waterfront until a monk from the monastery happens to appear in his motor boat. You must negotiate a fare with him. Once on the island, after a twenty-minute trip across one of the emptiest parts of the lagoon, you will find the total silence curiously unnerving.

When **Returning Home**
DO, when asked whether you enjoyed abroad, intone with a judicious chuckle: 'Travel broadens the seat.'

TOM AITKEN